PLAY THE GAME

SKIING

DOUGLAS GODLINGTON

BLANDFORD

First published in Great Britain in 1989
by Ward Lock Limited. Reprinted and revised in
1993 by Blandford, Villiers House, 41-47 Strand,
London WC2N 5JE.

A Cassell Imprint

Designed by Anita Ruddell
Figure drawings by Jerry Malone

Text set in Helvetica
by Hourds Typographica, Stafford, England
Printed and bound in Great Britain by
The Bath Press, Avon

British Library Cataloguing in Publication Data
Godlington, Douglas
    Skiing. Play the game (Ward Lock Limited)
    1. Skiing
    I. Title   II. Series
    796.93

ISBN 0 7137 2411 0

Acknowledgments

The publishers would like to thank Allsport for
permission to use the photographs on pages
2, 10/11, 67, 74/75, 78, and Coloursport for
those on pages 20, 31, 42/3 and 57.

Front Cover: Petra Kronberger

**Frontispiece: A proven all-round
world-class racer – Marc Girardelli**

SKIING

CONTENTS

FOREWORD

OVER the last few years there has been a marked increase in the popularity of ski holidays as a winter break – not only for those individuals and families who now have extra holiday time, but also for the large number of school parties going skiing. For a non-Alpine country such as Britain this development is also reflected in the escalating number of artificial ski slopes and specialist ski sports shops located all over the country to cater for the growing interest in skiing as a sport.

Skis, boots and bindings, too, have undergone change due to high-technology materials and production methods that have developed them into state-of-the-art equipment – efficient yet cosmetically part of modern imagery. This all contributes to the colourful scene that skiing presents, particularly attractive for those who are learning the basic steps.

However, skiing is not a 'natural' sport. You can't just jump on a pair of skis and expect to whizz off down an Olympic course. Skiing requires expert tuition through the different stages of learning to acquire the correct skills. Most skiers start by taking lessons in ski school and, as Director of a large ski school, I see many beginners each week progress from their first tentative slide to confident skiing down the easy slopes after just a few days. Learning in a ski school, with the guidance of well-trained staff, makes progressing through each new skill a fun experience and it is the ability to convey this enjoyment linked with progress that is the hallmark of an efficient and caring instructor.

The Association of Ski Schools in Great Britain carefully monitors those instruction standards to ensure that teaching methods are reviewed to make learning easier and safer. One of the rewards of being in ski school is the weekly test, awarded according to the proficiency level the pupil has attained. Having worked with the author of this book for many years in teaching people to ski – and in particular in connection with the Ski Test Award scheme – I know that any additional information that makes it easier for the learner to grasp the fundamentals of skiing is very welcome.

This is a book that fulfils that need. It is a book about the practical way to ski – the way in which skiing can be learned and enjoyed in safety. The descriptions of ski techniques are kept to clear simple explanation and are not complicated with over-technical jargon. For those new to the sport the book gives an insight into the skills required to become proficient, getting a feel for the skis and, most importantly, conveying what an exciting experience skiing can be.

Derek Brightman,
Director,
Cairdsport Ski Schools Ltd.

HISTORY & DEVELOPMENT OF SKIING

Tracing the origins of skiing has taken researchers more than 4000 years back in time when the use of some form of 'ski' was primarily a need for transport over a country clad in winter snows. The northern Scandinavian landscape, with its long winters, required the inhabitants to be able to move about during the long snowy months, and to be mobile on 'skis' must have been an integral part of life.

Various artefacts and early drawings have been found that record the use of some form of primitive, ski-like equipment. The Høting Ski, dug out of a peat bog in central Sweden and now in the Swedish Museum in Stockholm, has been dated to 2500 BC. Rock drawings depicting hunters on skis, found in northern Norway and Siberia, link the use of skis with Old Norse sagas, and the ancient writings of Far East legends tell of the need for man to hunt for food throughout the winter. However, these early 'skis' were more akin to snowshoes – some wide and short and others very long and narrow – used to prevent the wearer from sinking into deep snow.

The need for a more efficient means of sliding over the snow was probably brought about by the demands of military warfare — a mobile army in winter was a potential battle winner. It was during the thirteenth to seventeenth centuries, when wars and skirmishes took place between Scandinavian armies, that skis were developed into something like the shape we know today.

Until the nineteenth century, however, skis were used mainly as a means of transport, and any sporting event at a winter festival would have concentrated just on getting from one point to another across undulating countryside – the origins of cross-country skiing as it is known today.

Skiing as a sport owes its emergence to the activities of skiers from the Telemark district in Norway. On their local hillsides they practised jumping and then steering downhill in sweeping curves, discovering the thrill of swooping through the snow in elegant turns, which they called the 'Telemark' and 'Christiana'. These techniques formed the basis for modern Alpine downhill skiing by using turns to control and direct the skier's descent down a snowslope rather than going straight down.

One of these skiers from Telemark, Sondre Norheim, is credited with the fundamental

SKIING

An early skier

design shape of the skis used today, and with fixing the boots more securely to the skis with birch roots. From those days in the 1860s, when the first jumping competitions were organized and the first ski clubs formed in Norway, skiing was to spread throughout the world as a winter sport.

Meanwhile, the snowclad European slopes had only sporadic reports of any ski-like activity until the arrival of enthusiastic Norwegians carrying their wooden skis into the Alpine valleys in the late nineteenth century. Before the turn of the century they had taken their enthusiasm for skiing into North America and even into the Snowy Mountains of Australia. To meet the challenge of skiing down the steeper Alpine mountainsides, it was necessary to refine these Norwegian techniques. It was an Austrian, Matthias Zdarsky, who introduced the 'Stemm' and 'Snowplough', and later on Hannes Schneider, a fellow Austrian, who played a major part in the development of controlled ski-turning and instruction methods.

The foundations of skiing as a winter holiday began in the 1920s in the Alps, at Hannes Schneider's Ski School at St Anton. There they adopted a better boot-binding attachment to the ski which, together with the invention of the steel edge to the ski, made it both easier to control and, therefore, to learn to ski.

However, while a few large villages with hotels became established as winter sports resorts – offering skating, curling, sledging and now skiing – there was virtually no uphill transportation. For the most part, the only way up a hill was to walk up on skis, and climbing uphill was taken as part of the enjoyment! This led to organized ski touring being pioneered in Switzerland, as the more adventurous skiers began exploring the High Alps.

Mention should be made at this stage of two Englishmen who made a significant contribution to the establishment of skiing as a sport to be taken seriously. Vivian Caulfield studied the dynamics of skiing, explaining technique in his book *How to Ski*, published in 1910 and a revelation at the time. His analysis of the movements made to control skis is still applicable today. Arnold Lunn, later knighted for his services to skiing, had spent a long time living in Switzerland, and he decided that a different form of competition had to be created for Alpine skiing. His solution was to lay down the format and rules for Downhill and Slalom Racing. It became the foundation for all Alpine competitive skiing.

Organized skiing progressed into the 1930s with the installation of the first ski-lifts, which made learning to ski a deal quicker and less physically arduous. After World War II, rapid development of many Alpine Ski Centres took place throughout Austria and Switzerland, followed by the new concept of opening up virgin high mountain valleys with purpose-built resorts in the French Alps.

Since Zdarsky's first analysis of Alpine ski technique, and his development of a system of teaching people to ski, there have been many proposed styles and theories. To turn the skis in any form of fluent parallel swings down the slope, using the long wooden skis and low-cut leather boots of the pre-war skier, required a pronounced rotation of the whole body in order to impart a turning momentum through the legs to the skis. 'Rotational Skiing' became a standard style, a principle that dominated the progression of all those who learned to ski in the pre-war period. However, with the expansion of the winter holiday scene in the 1950s, ski technique was to erupt into strongly contested national styles as each of the Alpine ski countries adopted their own particular technique.

The changes in the methods and materials used in ski manufacture, and better boots and bindings, had a significant effect on the skier's performance, particularly in the field of competition. The way the top racers ski has always played a part in the development of ski technique. To have a racer on the winner's rostrum reflected not only the individual's competitive performance, but also that particular nation's lead in improving technique – with the added spin-off for marketing the equipment. In a small country such as Austria, where the ski-holiday industry was growing to become a major part of their economy, racing successes helped to present the country as a leader in the world of skiing.

The first radical shift in style and technique came in 1955 when Professor Stefan Kruckenhauser presented the Austrian Ski Teaching system. Based on body position over the skis, it reversed the upper body into a 'counter rotation' when making turns, and emphasized the turning of the skis in short turns called 'Wedeln'.

At the time this caused a revolution amongst the various ski nations, with those who saw the Austrian 'Wedel' technique as a move forward, and those who saw it only as a promotion of Austrian skiing and vehemently opposed the whole concept. But Kruckenhauser's system of learning to ski through stemming into parallel turns was adopted by many ski schools throughout the world, forming the first uniform approach to the method of instructing skiing.

National fervour had been aroused, however, and to counter the Austrian challenge as the 'ski masters' there were several new methods and styles promoted. The Italians stressed that a form of pre-rotation before making ski turns was the

The streamlined look of today's skier

answer; the American teaching method stressed 'Total Motion' of linked movements to turn the skis, and the Swiss maintained a middle line by building on the basic skills without any extremes of body position. All these techniques had the ultimate goal of performing ski turns with the skis parallel throughout the run down, as the hallmark of the competent skier.

The formation of the International Ski Instructors' Association brought about a more sensible approach to techniques and teaching methods. It was now possible to exchange new ideas and theories between those who were engaged in technique evaluation from all corners of the ski world.

From the 1970s to the present day, there has been a move toward a more uniform system of teaching. No matter from which ski school a person might choose to buy a lesson – in Japan, USA, or the Alps – the teaching system is very similar, particularly in the basic learning progressions. The indications are that the days of upholding hard doctrines on specific styles of skiing are over, and there is a more liberal attitude to the use of technique. Rather than saying this or that system is the best, it is possible to use something from all techniques at given moments when skiing.

Consequently ski technique has evolved to the point where, once the basic skills have been learned for controlling the skis, there are several ways in which technique can be used as the skier becomes more skilful. It is interesting to note that over the last decade, with the more open attitude to skiing, there has been an emergence of other forms of skiing – mono-skiing, surfboarding – and the upsurge in cross-country skiing as a healthy exercise away from the crowded pistes. As ski equipment continues to develop with modern technology, so also will the technique be adapted to ensure that skiing will always be a safe yet exhilarating sport.

Pirmin Zurbriggen of Switzerland was the leading World Cup skier for several years at the end of the 1980s.

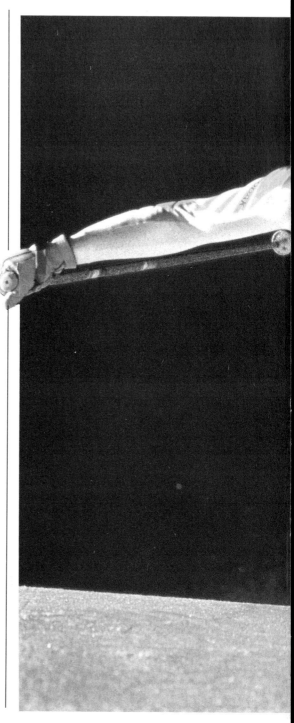

EQUIPMENT & TERMINOLOGY

To ski comfortably and efficiently, the skier must work as a complete unit with his or her equipment. It is essential that boots fit correctly, that bindings – the mechanism attaching the boots to the skis – are properly adjusted, and that skis are of the correct length and in good repair.

Any poor fitting of this equipment will have a detrimental effect on the link between legs and skis – too tight or too sloppy means that the skier will not be able to feel a proper response when making turning and controlling movements. At the same time there should be an adequate safety margin built into this link between skier and skis, so that the skis will become detached in the event of an awkward fall.

Choosing skis that are the correct type and length for your particular requirement is important, but it is equally important in the final link between skier and snow that the running surface and edges of the ski are well maintained so that they slide efficiently, and do not impair the sensation of skiing.

While having the correct hardware to go skiing, it is also necessary to dress sensibly for winter mountain weather. Ski wear must keep you warm and dry as a protection against extremes of wind and temperature, as well as preventing you from getting wet through when falling down as you learn to

ski. Seek the advice of the specialist ski shops when purchasing or renting equipment and clothing. Make sure that whatever you decide is practical and functional for the purpose, and not influenced by design trends.

Remember, you don't have to buy new equipment the first time you go skiing. You can either hire or buy second-hand equipment. There is always the remote chance you won't like skiing and buying new equipment makes it an expensive way of finding out.

Skis

The basic shape of the ski manufactured today may not have changed since the wooden skis made in Telemark by the nineteenth-century Norwegians, but the materials used are the products of space-age technology. In many respects the shape of a ski can be said to resemble a very elongated foot – widest at the toes and narrowest at the arch in the middle. If the geometric shape of the ski is much the same as that first made by Sondre Norheim, there have been significant changes in the functions of the ski. The arched curve of the ski, the camber, is designed to flex and distribute the skier's weight along the whole length, thicker in section at the centre under

The basic ski shape

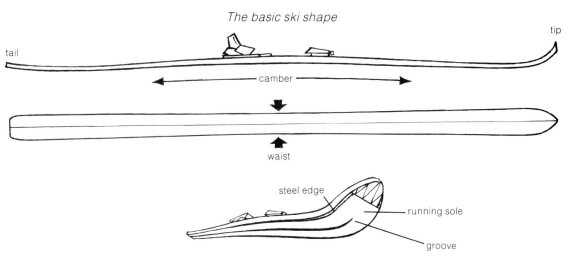

the skier's foot and binding mounting platform, thinning down in section towards the curved tip at the front and at the tail to the rear.

The most important function of the ski is its ability to steer and turn, yet at the same time travel in a straight line without wandering off-course. This is why the sides are cut into a waisted shape that helps the ski to steer in a curve, as well as flex into a reverse camber when the ski is tilted over on its edge.

The actual running surface of the ski on the snow, the sole, is made of a low-friction material to give smooth gliding over the snow. A shallow groove is machined down the centre of the sole to help it run straight, but some skis have no groove, making them easier to turn. The steel edges on the ski-sole are the working tools of the ski. These give a firm grip or 'bite' on the snow to ensure that the ski's steering and braking functions are effectively transmitted without excessive skidding.

Modern technology and manufacturing methods developed over the last few years mean that skis can be made for specific performance requirements, rather than the hit-and-miss design approach of earlier days. Today's skis are made from moulded laminations of a variety of plastics, fibre glass, alloy metals and low-friction polyethylenes, bonded together under precisely controlled manufacturing processes. This produces a ski that is durable and long-lasting, but keeps the built-in camber flex characteristic and provides resistance to twisting and excessive vibrations.

Choosing skis At first glance all skis look similar, but there are a number of differences which should be considered before choosing. Firstly, skis are made for several different requirements – for learners, competent recreational skiers, advanced keen skiers, and for the special performance needs of the racer.

The learner, choosing skis for the first time, will require a shorter ski that is easy to turn and control. They should be of a height that is approximately level with the top of your head or less. Competent skiers should choose skis that are 4in (10cm) above head height and of a flex pattern to suit their skiing ability.

The leading ski manufacturers all make excellent skis, and have similar model ranges across the different brands. Full information leaflets are issued on each type of ski and its

recommended use. In addition to this the ski magazines publish test reports on new ski products prior to each winter. A useful tip when you have purchased a new pair of skis, is to take note of the serial number and insure them against theft and breakage.

Maintaining skis It pays to look after your skis so that you will continue to get the best possible performance from them. The plastic sole is vulnerable to damage from rocks and loose stones, which can also blunt the steel edges. Scratches and scores can be filled in with P-tex repair candles, dripping the melted plastic into the damage and smoothing it out when set with a scraper. The edges can be sharpened by using a single-cut file flat across the sole, then taking off the side burrs by holding the file at right angles to the sole base. Edge-tuning tools are available to sharpen the edges to the correct angle.

A hot-wax application to the skis will make them run better, especially in new snow conditions, and will also help to protect the running surface. There are a range of waxes available to suit various snow conditions, and they can be purchased in block form and in tubes. Any reputable ski shop will give a ski-tuning and waxing service as well as repairing more serious damage.

Ski bindings

The ski binding is the device which holds the boot firmly on to the ski. The mechanism is designed to grip the boot through all the stresses and strains of normal skiing, yet 'release' when subjected to abnormal twisting loads or pressure that may otherwise injure the skier.

Most binding systems consist of two units fixed to the ski and adjustable to the size of

Beginners should choose skis that are approximately level with the top of their head.

the boot. There is a toe-piece that grips the front of the boot and a heel-piece clamping down the boot heel. In the event of a critical loading on the boot that could cause injury, the toe-piece twists sideways and the heel-piece opens if the skier falls forward.

However, the release mechanisms need to have built-in shock absorbers to take the stresses and loads of normal skiing without inadvertently opening up. Adjustment of the release setting on the binding is made according to the D.I.N. International Standard loading scale, numbered 1 to 10, which is calculated according to the skier's weight and ability. Learners and light-weight skiers use low numbers, and more proficient skiers belong further up the scale. Use an approved ski shop to fit and adjust bindings properly.

Incorporated into the binding system is a braking device that retracts when the boot is fitted, but springs out if the ski is released from the boot and stops the ski from sliding off down the mountain. The brakes also clip together to hold the skis when carrying them. If the bindings do not have stoppers built-in, use retaining straps to avoid losing the ski. It is important to keep bindings lubricated, and to make regular checks on the fixing screws, adjustment parts and the release setting.

Choosing bindings All the main types of ski binding are manufactured to approved standards, and in terms of safety are all very similar. The cost of various models is based on the materials used and the skier's particular requirements.

Ski boots

Of all the skier's equipment, boots are the most important item. A correct fit is essential to transfer the controlling movements from leg to ski without movement loss, and to hold the foot comfortably for the ski.

The modern plastic boot is made in two parts: a rigid outer shell moulded in plastic material, and a softer foam-filled inner boot that cushions the foot. There are many different designs and several opening systems, all fastened with adjustable clips to obtain a final snug fit onto the foot. The boot soles all conform to the international

*The ski boot and entry
into the binding mechanism*

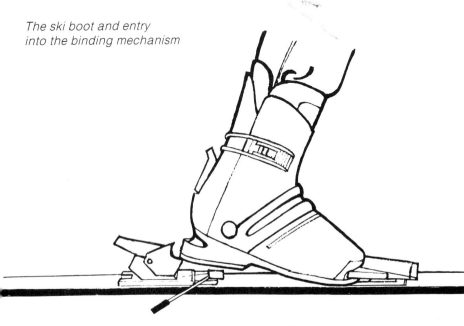

standard shape to fit correctly into the bindings.

The design of the modern boot gives a rigid support to the foot and lower leg, preventing any sideways ankle movement as when edging the ski, but allowing for some forward flexing movement without lifting the heel inside the boot. They are not designed to walk any distance in. However, for short distances, walking is made easier by releasing the grip of the upper shaft of the boot.

Choosing boots   There are various models to suit the different skiing categories from beginner to high-performance racer. It is usual to measure the foot wearing a single pair of ski socks. Check that the fit allows for some movement of the toes, while gripping the heel firmly when the ankle is flexed forward. Walk around and flex the feet inside the boots; the shin and ankle area should be comfortably gripped. Any small pressure points can be either adjusted or customized by the technical staff of the shop. Some boots have additional facilities for canting over to suit the individual's foot shape, making edging more positive.

Once you have a comfortable pair of boots, treat them carefully. Don't walk excessively in them or you will wear out the soles, and take the inners out when drying.

Ski poles

Ski poles are used as a support for walking and stepping round, and as a balancing aid when skiing. For the proficient skier they are used as part of the technique for turning.

They are manufactured from tapered light alloy with a plastic handle, a snow disc or basket and a steel tip. The choice between poles lies in the handle design: most have wrist straps to retain a grip on the pole, while others have a moulded plastic grip around the hand. Check for the correct length of pole by gripping the vertically inverted pole under the basket; with the handle on the

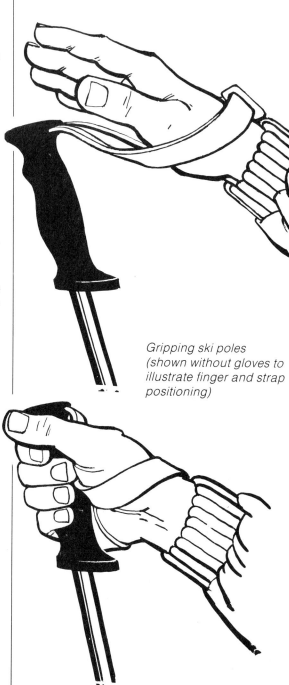

Gripping ski poles (shown without gloves to illustrate finger and strap positioning)

floor the forearm should be parallel with the ground.

Ski wear

Mountain weather can be very changeable, especially under extremes of winter conditions, so it is advisable always to dress on the cautious side. To keep warm and dry, clothing should be windproof and waterproof, preferably insulated against freezing temperatures, yet comfortable enough not to restrict movement.

Dress in a three-layer system: (1) thermal underwear and long-johns that can breathe and draw away moisture; (2) a mid-layer of polo-neck T-shirt and sweater to absorb moisture, to which further thin layers can be added as necessary; (3) then finally you wear an outer 'shell' layer of wind and waterpoof fabrics.

Ski clothes

The most expensive investment is the outer garments, particularly with ski clothing now part of the designer fashion scene. However, the practical value of a ski jacket, trousers, bib-salopettes, or a complete one-piece suit, is the first consideration when buying. Weatherproof laminated fabrics that allow microscopic ventilation have revolutionized ski-wear, as have the inner layers of lightweight insulation materials.

Check the garment for sensible design of collar, pockets and zips, and see that the fabric is tough enough to stand up to skiing's wear and tear – all points that come before the attraction of the latest colour schemes.

Ski wear accessories   The extremities of the body lose heat quickly. The head, hands and feet can soon get cold, especially if poor-quality clothing is worn. **A woollen ski hat or insulated cap**, large enough to adequately cover the head, is important, and for young children skiing on busy pistes a crash helmet is recommended.

Keeping hands warm means going for good-quality **gloves or mittens**. Leather is still the first choice of material for wear and general durability, and gloves should be well insulated with extra wear protection on the palm and thumb areas. For extreme cold conditions a pair of silk or thermal material inner gloves are recommended.

Ski socks are made with an inner loopstitch lining for warmth, and to avoid any discomfort from pressure of the boots they should reach above the top of the boot.

Ski goggles are used to protect the eyes from wind, blizzard and sun-glare and for improving vision in poor visibility. Models available vary from those with a single lens to more expensive double-lens models that lessen the chance of fogging-up. Use yellow or rose-tinted lenses for bad light conditions. **Sunglasses** are for good weather with strong sunlight reflecting off the snow; use a good polarized dark lens, large enough to cover the whole eye area.

Strong sunlight also means protecting the neck and face from possible burn by using a recommended **suncream**. Don't forget that lips can become sore, so protect with a **lip salve**.

Important note   Being cold – a chilled body or even cold hands – leads to a reduction in concentration in the first instance, and in severe weather conditions to more serious hypothermia problems. Learning to ski demands all your concentration, and being sensibly dressed and warm is essential to get the most progress and enjoyment from skiing.

Cross-country equipment

With the resurgences of cross-country skiing as a popular winter exercise activity there have been changes in equipment design. The sport of cross-country skiing is essentially walking on skis, a kind of ramble over snow-covered countryside or along an Alpine valley. The techniques are simple and quick to learn in the basic form, but get more specialized for those who want to take the sport more seriously or go in for competitive racing. Because the terrain used is more gentle – up and down easy slopes that require less edge control against speed – the equipment used is much lighter than for Alpine skiing.

Skis are longer and narrower, designed to follow a track and glide forward in a straight line, although it is possible to snowplough and make parallel turns. Telemark skis have steel edges and are designed to make the elegant sweeping Telemark turns of the loose-heel devotees.

The major innovation in cross-country skiing has been the fish-scale sole. Traditionally a grip-wax is used to obtain a push and glide forward and for climbing. It requires some time to prepare the skis and the wax must be correct for the particular snow conditions. Nowadays, a fish-scale

Cross-country skiing

pattern is moulded into the ski sole under the foot and this eliminates the need for grip-wax; it also does away with the complications of getting the waxing right.

Lightweight boots, fitted into a small toepiece which leaves the heel free to lift, are another feature of the equipment. Longer poles are used, and these give a better push forward with each gliding step.

Clothing, too, is lightweight: cross-country skiers wear thin layers which they add to or take off as required. The outer layer is always a thin windproof and waterproof shell.

TERMINOLOGY

You are now familiar with the equipment you need to get on to the piste. But before we go through the all-important skiing techniques, you should familiarize yourself with the terms you will encounter both in this book and when you get out on the slopes:

Equipment

Binding   Toe and heel mechanism for fixing the boot on to the ski. It is equipped with a built-in adjustable release function.

Camber   The curved arch of the ski designed to distribute the skier's weight.

Canting   Adjustment of the boot sole relative to the ski to obtain a better edge-grip.

D.I.N.   The rating scale for release binding settings, and other standardized safety features on equipment.

Edges   The steel edges down the sides of the ski's running surface.

Flex pattern   The distribution of flexing stiffness along the length of the ski.

Mono ski   Wide single ski for both feet, primarily for use in deep snow.

Poles   Ski sticks; tapered tube poles used for balance, and as an aid to climbing and turning.

Reverse camber   The shape taken by the ski when it is under load during turning.

Short ski   Skis of a shorter than normal length, used in the learning progression.

Shovel   The forepart of the ski including the tip.

Side   The waisting shape of the ski to assist turning. See Waisting.

Ski brake   Device attached with the binding for arresting the ski should the binding release.

Sole   The under running surface of polyethylene material within the steel edges.

Torsional stiffness   Degree of resistance to twisting along the ski length.

Waisting   The narrower centre section of the ski, formed by the side-cut.

Waxes   Applied to the sole of the ski to improve gliding according to snow conditions. Either melted on hot or rubbed on. Also refers to grip-waxes applied to Nordic skis.

Ski technique

Angulation   The shape of the body used to control turning and edge-grip – leaning out from the slope with the upper body, the hips and legs leaning inwards.

Anticipation   The pre-turning of the body before initiating a turning movement.

Basic swing   Turning manoeuvre beginning with a plough and finishing with a parallel swing.

Carving   Turning and steering the skis with minimum sideways skid.

Christiania   'Christie' turns are made with the skis in a parallel position.

Compression   Bending the legs to absorb bumps, and initiate turns.

Down-flex   The downward flexing of the egs – a hip, knee, ankle-bending movement.

Dynamic balance   Maintaining balance control while in motion.

Edge change   The changing over from one edge to the other as the skis turn.

Edge-set   The degree of edge grip or bite on the snow.

Fall-line   The line of least resistance down a slope – the steepest angle.

Herringbone   Stepping uphill with the ski-tips apart and the tails together.

Inside ski   The ski on the inside of a turning arc.

Inward lean   The leaning inward of the legs, or body, to the inside of a turn.

Lower ski   The ski to the downhill side of the skier.

Outside ski   The ski to the outside of a turning arc.

Parallel turn or swing   A turning arc across the slope with the skis in a parallel position to one another.

Pivot   Rotating or twisting action by the legs to turn the skis.

Plough   With the skis angled out in a 'V' form, as when snowploughing.

Pole-plant   The action of placing a pole in the snow to aid turning.

The Canadian star skier Rob Boyd.

SKIING

Pressure   The application of the skier's weight pressure on the ski.

Schuss   Skiing straight downhill without braking.

Short swings   Short-radius turns in a continuous action down steep slopes.

Sideslip   Releasing the edge-grip to slip or skid sideways downhill.

Skidding   Allowing the skis to skid sideways, usually when turning.

Snowplough   Basic controlling technique, the skis in a 'V' form from the tips.

Stance   The body position over the moving skis, the joints flexed.

Steering   The guiding of the skis (or ski) in a given turn or direction.

Stem   Moving one ski out at an angle from the tip, onto its inside edge.

Straight run   Skiing straight down the fall-line with skis parallel.

Swing   Turning the skis in a curving arc with skis parallel.

Track   (1) The mark in the snow left by the skis; also (2) directing the skis.

Traverse   Skiing across the slope at an angle to the fall-line.

Turn   Changing direction with the skis, usually through the fall-line.

Turn phases   Any ski turn has three distinct phases through which the skier applies the movements of the particular technique:
   Preparation phase – making movements to get ready for turning the skis.

Initiation phase – the moment the skis are turned into the change of direction.
Steering phase – all the turning movements have been completed and the rest of the turn is steered round the slope into the next turn.

Unweighting   A brief reduction of the weight pressure on the skis to enable the initiation of turning movements by upward extension of the body.

Upper ski   The ski to the uphill side of the skier.

Wedge   As for snowploughing, this usually refers to skis placed at a narrow plough angle.

Weight change   The shifting of the skier's weight pressure from one ski to the other, particularly when initiating a turn.

Weighting   The application of the skier's weight pressure to the ski(s).

Around the ski resort

Alpine skiing   Term used for sport of downhill skiing using lifts, etc., as distinct from Nordic skiing using free-heel equipment for cross-country and touring.

Artificial snow   Man-made snow blown out onto the ski runs.

Avalanche   (German *Lawine*) Breakaway and slide of a mass of snow – dangerous areas which should be avoided.

Courtesy code   Guidelines for safe skiing – the Skier's Highway Code.

Downhill race   A timed speed event over a prepared course with few control markers, usually over a descent in vertical height of 800 to 1000 metres; speeds over 60mph. Crash helmets must be worn.

EQUIPMENT · & · TERMINOLOGY

Gates Marker poles for race courses.

Giant slalom race A more open and longer slalom race, with the gates spread wider apart. Run twice.

Lifts Uphill transport for skiers can be found in several forms:

 Nursery tow – small ski-tow pulling the skier who holds on to a rope or handle.
 T-bar – pulls two skiers up side by side, keeping the skis in the track.
 Poma lift – single bar and button, pulls the skier uphill; most have an automatic

Giant slalom race

bar-dispensing action.

Chairlift – the skier is carried sitting in a chair attached to a cable.

Using the above lifts requires attention when moving into the correct position before take-off, and then care in getting off at the top. Take note of all the operating signs.

Gondola and cable cars – small and large cabin lifts.

Moguls   Rounded bumps formed on ski runs by the constant turning of skis scouring the snow away.

Nordic skiing   Cross-country skiing as developed in the Nordic Scandinavian countries. It covers ski wandering, langlauf racing, Biathlon racing, Citizens Events, Telemark Skiing, and Ski Touring. This is also referred to as 'loose-heel' skiing, because the boot is only secured by a toe-piece, making it possible to ascend as well as go down.

Piste   The ski run – the area prepared for skiing down.

Piste-basher   A large tracked vehicle used for grooming the snow.

Ski patrol   (German *Rettungsdienste*, French *Pisteurs*) service responsible for patrolling the ski area, summoned in the event of an accident.

Ski run   The prepared run, marked and patrolled, graded according to difficulty. Graded and marked as follows:

    Green – easy
    Blue – moderately easy
    Red – difficult
    Black – very difficult

Ski trail   As Ski run, but usually a trail cut through trees.

Slalom race   A ski race over a steep prepared course of closely set gates (55 to 75 over 200m vertical descent). Run twice.

Super-G race   A type of downhill race with more control gates. Run once only.

BASIC
SKIING
TECHNIQUE

Whatever your reasons for learning to ski – from having a winter holiday to keeping fit – it will be necessary to learn basic principles. How quickly you become accustomed to the skis and get the feel for applying controlling techniques will depend largely on the individual. If you are reasonably fit and already able to skate or skateboard, or take part in similar balancing sports, then progress will be quick. However, if you are not active, then it will take a little longer to become proficient.

There are broadly three stages in the initial process of learning to ski

(1) getting used to the equipment,

(2) applying elementary controlling movements, and finally

(3) practising on easy ski runs.

Through these stages the skier will learn the basic skills necessary to apply ski technique and progress onto more proficient forms of skiing.

Getting the feel of the equipment

Wearing ski boots for the first time can be a strange feeling. That's why, if you buy your own boots, it pays to get the feel of them at home before stepping out onto the snow. The grip and restriction on the foot of the boot, plus the weight and awkwardness of the skis when they are fastened, are new sensations that you must get used to quickly.

To put your skis on, first choose a flat area of snow, place the skis down side by side, clean off the snow from the boot soles and step into the binding, toe first. Press the heel down hard to lock the boot securely to the ski. If it isn't fitting square to the ski, release the heel catch and check that all the snow is cleaned off the boot sole. It helps to lean on the ski poles while getting the skis on. If there is the slightest angle of slope, the skis will want to slide, so make sure they are across the slope. It is easier to put the downhill-side ski on first.

To get accustomed to your new restriction of movement, slide the skis backward and forward, lift alternate feet, hop the tails off the snow, and step round in a circle leaving

SKIING

Carrying skis – don't forget to be careful of what is in front and behind you!

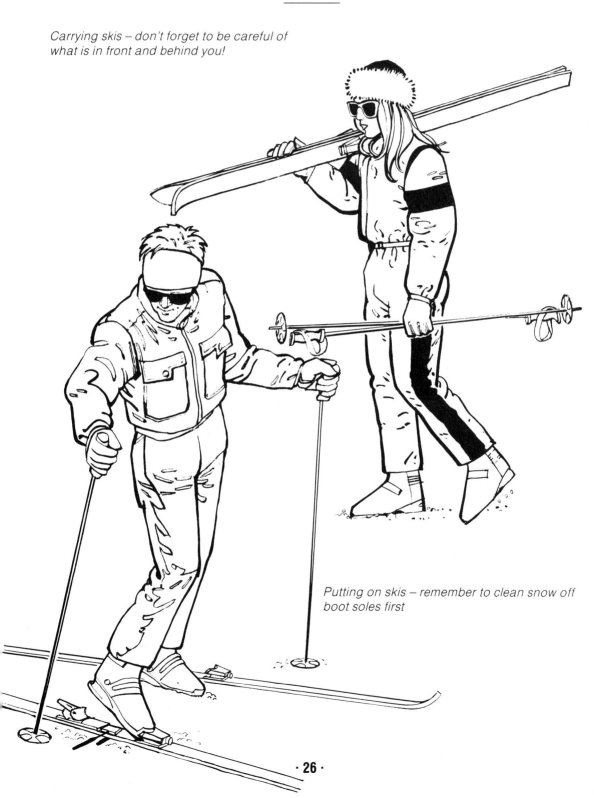

Putting on skis – remember to clean snow off boot soles first

a 'star' pattern. These are all exercises to get you used to the feel of what you can and can't do with skis fixed to your legs – crossing your feet for instance!

Now slide the skis. Walk forward by sliding one foot at a time. It's impossible to lift the heel so the action is a kind of shuffling step. Push on the poles to try and get the skis to glide over the snow with each step. The rhythm is that of the normal walking action,

left ski with right arm forward, etc. Make a track to follow if the ground is suitable, round in a circle, stepping out of the way of any obstacles. This teaches you to feel the sliding sensation under your feet and the limitations imposed by the length of the skis. Try pushing and sliding forward on both skis together, using your poles to propel you forward.

Star turn

SKIING

Falling down is part of skiing. If you lose balance, allow your legs to relax and sit down to one side in the snow. Resist the temptation to reach down with your hand to stop the fall, as it is possible to sprain your thumb or wrist.

Getting back up again requires a little thought. Skis have to be brought back parallel together, close to the body, so that as soon as you push off from the snow with your hand, you can lean forward over your boots and then stand up.

If you fall on a slope, then it is important to make sure the skis are across the slope on the downhill side, so they do not slide off as you attempt to stand up. You can use your poles to help push upright. They must be placed close to your body so that you can lever yourself forward over your boots as you get up.

If it is still difficult to get upright again, take off the ski nearest to the side you are sitting, and stand up on that leg, replacing the ski once the snow has been cleaned off.

When getting up from a fall, lean well forward with head over boots

TECHNIQUE

Side-stepping, using uphill edges to grip

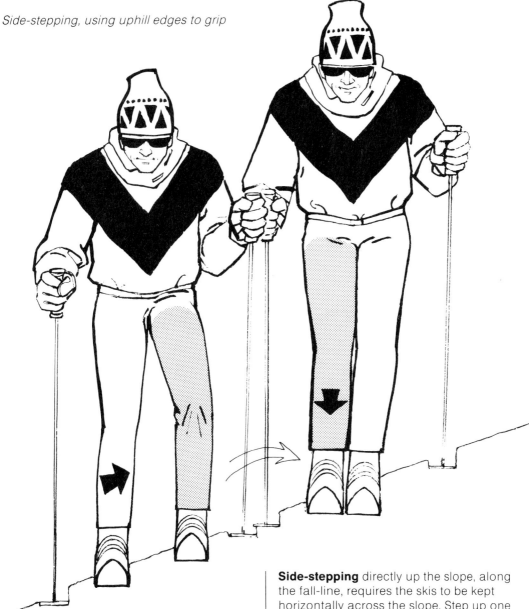

Gliding downhill in balance is the first skiing skill to acquire. Choose a gentle slope that has a safe runout on to a flat area. But first it may be necessary to climb up the hill, and this too requires some attention about how you use your skis to step uphill.

Side-stepping directly up the slope, along the fall-line, requires the skis to be kept horizontally across the slope. Step up one ski at a time, while using the poles for support. The skis have to be pressed into the snow on their uphill edges to obtain a grip. To obtain the edge-grip, press both knees sideways in toward the slope, taking small steps like climbing up a staircase sideways.

It is also possible to walk and climb

SKIING

Basic running stance: left shows normal stance, right shows flexing to absorb uneven ground

straight up the slope by opening out the tips of the skis well apart, to stop sliding backwards. Step with boots apart, toes out at an angle and edged inward to make the skis grip on the snow.

Using the poles for support in the snow downhill, make alternate steps forward to clear the tails of the skis, pressing down on the inside edge with each step. This is called the **herringbone step**. Step round across the slope while leaning for support on the poles downhill.

Straight running is the first taste of skiing directly downhill. It requires the skier to assume a stance over the skis that can be adjusted to meet any changes in the run of the skis that will affect balance. This **basic running stance** is the fundamental dynamic

position from which all skiing movements are made, so it is important to get the correct feel for this stance before moving off.

While standing still, boots and skis comfortably apart, flex-bend the hips, knees and ankle joints slightly, lean the upper body slightly forward and carry arms and poles out to the side. The purpose of holding a flexed stance like this is that it is a 'ready position'. From here you can bend more or stretch up, lean side to side, and take front and rear shocks as the skis slide.

Step the skis round into the fall-line,

Franz Heinzer bursts over a crest during the Alpine Ski World Championships.

leaning on your poles placed downhill, and, when you are ready, simply lean forward and allow yourself to slide off. Once underway, the whole body should be relaxed and not tensed up, with the weight even on both feet. Keep the arms out to the side as a balancing aid. Allow the skis to glide out on to flat ground, or even on to a slight rise to slow up, then climb back up the slope and practise these runs, or schusses, several times.

You can test your reflex responses to staying up in balance by doing several exercises while on the move. Reach up and down, lean forward and back against your boots, lift the tail of each ski in turn so that you glide for a brief moment on one ski only.

Find a slope with a hump and hollow to ski over, bending and stretching your legs to act as shock absorbers, as well as feeling any slowing down or speeding up of the skis. Don't rely on your boots to keep you upright, particularly by sitting and leaning on the high back of the boot. Reach and look ahead, feel for the sliding sensation through the soles of your feet.

To slow down, try spreading the tails of the skis apart into a 'V' shape, turning your heels outward so that the skis begin to **snowplough** against the snow. As you push the backs of the skis apart, the sole of the ski will tilt over toward its inside edge, this creates the snowplough resistance as the skis brush over the snow. The wider your legs spread out to increase the snowplough angle, the more resistance against the snow and braking effect this will have on your skis. It requires care and attention, holding the basic stance, legs flexed, and it is essential that both legs work equally, helping you to develop a feel for the inside edges that will slow you down.

The snowplough is not only the technique for the learner to control speed, but is also used by the expert skier when it is necessary to ski slowly. However, not everyone finds it easy at first to ski down with legs apart, and it requires practice to get accustomed to the feeling.

From the top of the easy slope, set off as before in the basic running stance, only this time with the ski tails slightly apart in a small wedge or plough position. The ski soles are flat on the snow so there should be very little resistance to gliding downhill. Now push the heels wider and feel the braking action against the edges.

Practise this several times, opening and closing the snowplough angle to feel the braking and speeding-up effect. Work on both skis by bending and straightening the legs until you feel comfortably able to control the skis.

You can test your snowplough control ability by choosing or marking a spot on the slope at which to stop, bending and lowering your body between the skis as they widen to get the most braking effect. If the snow is too deep, or hard to push against, then the skis will have to be stepped one at a time to one side in order to slow down. Stepping the skis to change direction is a good exercise to try in any case.

Elementary turning control – snowplough turns

Once the feeling for gliding and holding the snowplough stance has been acquired, then the skier can move on to more controlling movements necessary to become fully mobile. Alpine skiing concentrates on the skier's ability to turn the skis in a series of curving arcs from one way to the other, across the line of descent. This is the way you control your speed downhill.

The snowplough enables the learner to make this change of direction at slow speed, and at the same time acquire a feeling for more skiing skills. In the straight snowplough downhill, the skier's weight is distributed evenly on both skis. If more weight pressure is applied to one ski only then that ski will begin to steer in the direction it is pointing, and if the skis are held in the plough angle the skier will eventually turn across the line of the slope and stop.

The snowplough – pushing out the ski heels onto the inside edges

This is the principle of snowplough turns. Pressing down on the right ski will turn you across the slope to the left; to turn to the right, put more weight on the left ski. To apply this pressure effectively on the turning ski, flex down more on that leg, feeling for the pressure on the inside of the foot down to the inside edge of the ski. Holding the weight pressure down on the turning leg is helped by leaning slightly sideways over the ski with the upper body, bending from the hips. Try small turns out of the fall-line in both directions to get the initial feel of the skis skidding round.

From the top of the practice slope make snowplough turns by applying steering pressure first to one ski, turning out of the downhill descent, then straightening up the body to change the weight pressure over to the other ski. As the skis turn downhill again, the new turning leg should be flexed down to steer the ski along its inside edge.

Concentrate on holding the skis out in the correct snowplough angle the whole time. Widen the plough if the skis go too fast, lessen the angle and let the skis glide if you are going too slowly.

Practise linking snowplough turns together, developing confidence to make the skis go where you want. Feel the inside edge under the ball of the foot and get more rhythm as you steer from one turn into the next. Most people have a natural stronger side – usually right hand and foot – so making rhythmical turning patterns will help to match the weaker leg without consciously having to work harder on that particular side. It also helps to relax and relieve any tension by counting out loud to the rhythmic pattern of the turn – 'One-and-two-and-three-and . . .'

Add a little more to the practice by reaching well to the side by the outer hand and pole, putting positive weight over the turning ski. Try skiing down with the hands on top of the knees. Press hard down on the turning leg, pushing the knee toward the tip to aid the steering effect.

The snowplough turn – weighting and steering the outside leg and ski

As your snowplough turns become more proficient and controlled, you can think about adding a twisting of the feet as the skis steer and skid round the slope. Once again, some learners will grasp the technique for turning more quickly than others. Over-concentrating or fear of shooting off down the slope can produce tenseness in the body, thus blocking what is a fairly straightforward sliding stance and leg movement. By introducing an objective turning challenge, such as a few poles or snowballs spaced out down the slope, attention can be diverted to the new

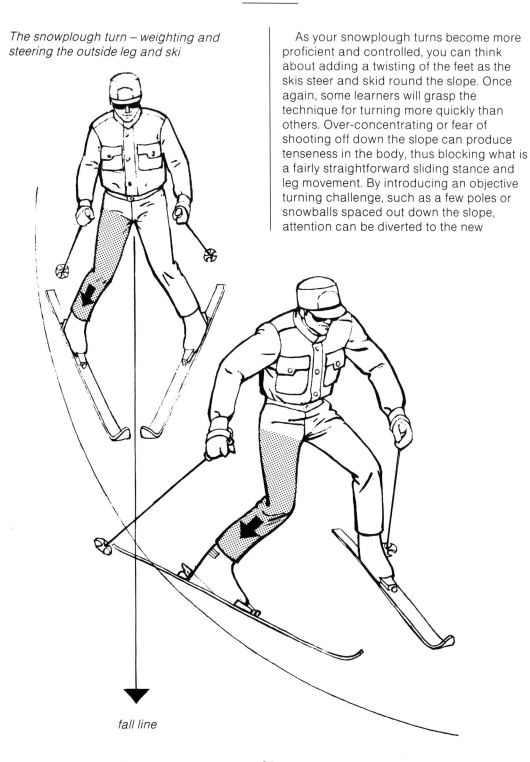

fall line

challenge. Focussing this attention, try steering only with the feet round the markers.

Having got to this stage of controlling your skis and turning down an easy gradient slope, it is time to practise on a longer nursery slope where there are simple ski tows. While working on your turning technique, and avoiding other skiers, remember always to look ahead at the snow. Move out of the way of awkward-looking bumps and ridges, and rough patches of snow that may cause problems as you slide over them.

Using the ski-tow takes the hard work out of getting back uphill. It gives you more time and energy to apply the first principles of controlling your skis – being able to hold your balance while in motion, to move your balance to shift your weight to either ski, and the important skill of feeling for the inside edge of the ski for steering.

Riding up ski-tows is also good practice for guiding and steering the skis. It's like skiing uphill – leaning back to take the pull of the lift as you direct the skis up the tow-track. It also gives you time to watch other skiers, looking at how they turn and steer their skis as they go by down the slope – and noting their mistakes!

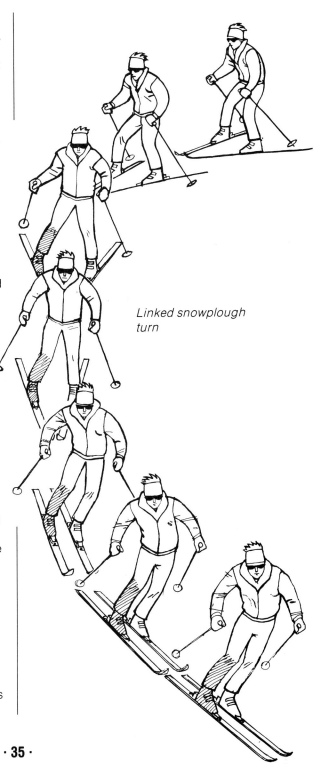

Linked snowplough turn

Easy runs and parallel skidding

Making snowplough turns enables the novice to learn the basic skills for ski control at slow speed. With the feet spread apart in the angled-out plough shape is a very stable stance for gliding steadily over the snow. Both inside edges are ready for use in the plough position to keep the skis moving slowly or turning, giving time for the learner to think what movements have to be made with the legs and body to control the skis.

However, snowploughing all the time can be tiring. Having your legs spread apart is not a natural position, especially when you want the skis to slide faster. To allow the skis to glide more quickly and obtain more

SKIING

Traversing – lower legs toward the slope, keep head over lower ski to grip the uphill edges

efficient steering, you should now bring the inside ski into use, so that you have two edges to steer and brake with.

Once you have become confident at linking your snowplough turns together, there are new techniques to learn so that both skis can be made to work for you.

Traversing across the slope When skiing across the slope for any distance, it isn't necessary to hold the plough or 'wedge' position with the skis. Both skis can be pointed in the same direction to hold the track or traverse line. This means adjusting the basic stance over the skis so that they glide on their uphill edges. This provides a grip on the snow to track them across, rather than straight down, the hill.

The straight running stance is adjusted to make provision for standing sideways to the slope. Do this by pushing the uphill ski, knee, hip and shoulder forward, at least half a boot length. At the same time, more weight is applied to the downhill ski, helped by leaning the upper body out over the ski. To make the skis edge and grip into the snow, the knees and hips are pressed toward the slope, tilting the boots and skis over, just as when sidestepping uphill. As when skiing straight down, the skis are placed comfortably apart under the hips, to give a more stable position when underway – the 'open stance' for practical skiing.

Now you can vary your skiing downhill by linking snowplough turns with a traverse across the slope before making the next turn. This will give you a rest from holding the snowplough and give you a feeling for guiding the uphill ski on its outside edge.

To stop when traversing, simply push the tail of the lower ski downhill into a small plough-angle. You must flex the leg more on this ski to obtain a good edge-grip as it begins to brake and slow you down.

Try some test exercises to see if you are holding the traverse stance correctly. With the skis parallel, moving at a shallow angle across the slope to keep the gliding speed steady, lift the tail of the upper ski off the snow and glide for a moment on the lower ski. This is a test of balance and to see if you are able to place more weight on the lower edged ski. It helps to balance better by opening your arms wider as you lift the ski.

Next try lifting the upper ski totally off the snow, stepping it to the uphill side, still on a parallel tracking line. Change the weight on to this ski and step up the downhill ski into the new tracking line. Make a series of small steps one at a time, like sidestepping on the move. The test here is for feeling the edge-hold as you step from one ski to the other, and for co-ordinating your movements while gliding forward.

You are now at the stage to try **Easy Ski Runs**, those marked Green or Yellow. The Ski Area Map will show where these are located, and which lifts serve them. Use the practice on these runs to allow the skis to glide without too much braking. Narrow the snowplough angle down to a small wedge to reduce excessive braking on the inside edges, and to make it less tiring on your legs. Change the rhythm of turning to include some traverses that link the turns together. To make a snowplough turn from the traverse, slide the uphill ski out into the plough angle from the tip, feeling the ski skid over to its inside edge under your foot. Now the skis are ready to be turned in the opposite direction.

Remember the outside ski is always the main steering ski when making any ski turn, and that as you turn downhill the skis will speed up. They will slow down again as you turn through the fall-line, back across the slope. This will become an instinctive feeling as you get more experience. However, for these first runs, where the snow slope may have undulating terrain, it is important to bear this in mind and be ready to adjust your balance if the skis suddenly accelerate.

The Easy Ski Run is the first taste of real skiing, but in the elation of having 'arrived' don't forget there are certain guidelines that have to be observed when skiing downhill, just like the Highway Code for driving. Look out for other skiers joining you in moving downhill. Don't let the skis go out of control. Keep clear of other skiers to avoid collisions, and if you want to stop for a rest (or put the skis back on after a fall), move to a safe place on the snow, usually at the side of the piste.

Also keep a lookout for the Piste Direction Signs. In a busy ski resort they will be numbered, so make sure you stay on your easy run and do not stray off down a World Cup Slalom Course!

Finally, at this stage it is very easy to get carried away with your progress and do too many practice runs without realizing how tiring this can be, not only from the physical effort, but from concentrating on 'thinking technique'. The obvious rule here is to stop when you feel tired. Don't be persuaded to take one more last run if you are weary – that's when accidents happen.

Side-slipping and skidding the skis

parallel   Being able to use the edges of the ski efficiently is an important skiing skill, and is a major part of the learning progression. The steel-edges are the working part of the 'ski-tool' that allow the skis to effectively grip the snow surface. Control of the effective angle of edge-grip is made by the feet and lower leg securely clipped into the ski boots. Any sideways movement of the legs across the ski will have an immediate effect on the grip of the ski-edge in the snow. Pressing the knees into the slope will increase the grip and moving the knees outward to the downhill side will reduce the edge-grip.

Developing this edge-grip feel is essential for progressing toward making turns with the skis in a parallel position, rather than continually snowploughing. First of all try from a gentle traverse, in the ready stance. Release the edge-grip by moving the knees outward, down the slope. This action is done only by the lower leg and boots rolling the skis off their edges, feeling them slip sideways with the soles of the feet as gravity pulls the skis downhill. Control the slipping motion by flexing the legs more to sink down over the skis. At the same time, help to maintain stability by pushing the upper ski well forward and facing down the slope. Stop by pressing the knees back in toward the slope to regain an edge-grip.

In practice, side-slipping is used for slowing down, allowing the skis to slip broadside across the snow and braking with sideways scraping of the edges against the snow-surface. On steep pitches where turning could be difficult, height can be lost by using a controlled side-slip. It can also be used when moving down in the line of a lift queue.

Look for an even snow slope to try your first side-slip exercises, and remember to

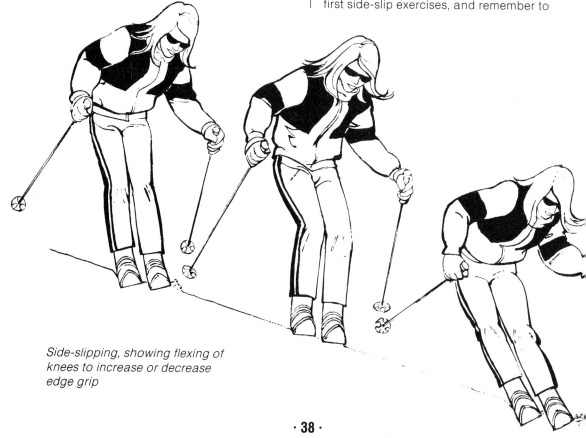

Side-slipping, showing flexing of knees to increase or decrease edge grip

Parallel skidding across the slope.

make them to both right and left traverse lines, working on your weaker side to get the feel of control. To help you get the feel of this, first try pushing yourself downhill with your poles planted in the snow on the uphill side to start the skis slipping.

Skidding turn across the slope   This is the next important step – converting the feeling of 'edge-play' (learned from side-slipping) into direct use when turning. Instead of slipping down and across the slope, it is now necessary to be able to steer both skis in a wide curved track across the snow.

Making a parallel skidded swing requires a little more speed than side-slipping. Start from a steeper line, traversing in the ready stance – feet apart and more weight to the

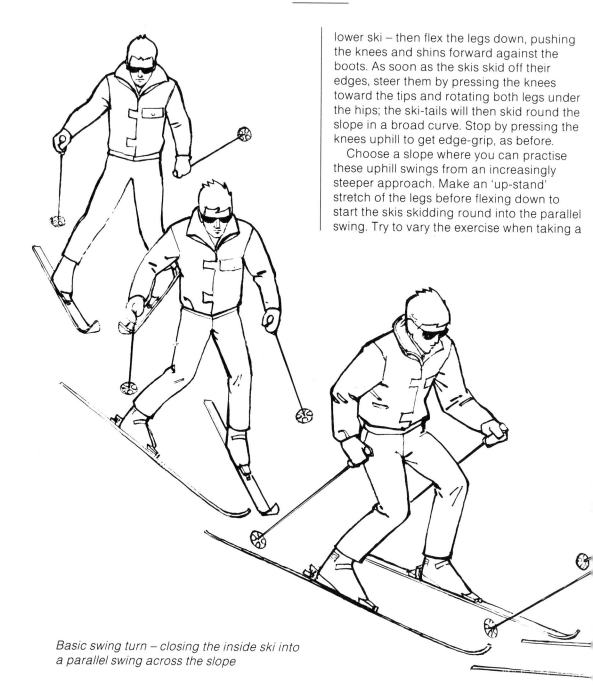

lower ski – then flex the legs down, pushing the knees and shins forward against the boots. As soon as the skis skid off their edges, steer them by pressing the knees toward the tips and rotating both legs under the hips; the ski-tails will then skid round the slope in a broad curve. Stop by pressing the knees uphill to get edge-grip, as before.

Choose a slope where you can practise these uphill swings from an increasingly steeper approach. Make an 'up-stand' stretch of the legs before flexing down to start the skis skidding round into the parallel swing. Try to vary the exercise when taking a

Basic swing turn – closing the inside ski into a parallel swing across the slope

run on an easy slope. Make short stop swings to longer curved turns, linked one to another across the slope. Avoid the temptation to throw the hips out from the traverse line to start the ski-tails skidding downhill. The turning is all done by rotating the legs under the body, keeping the hips to the uphill side and angling the upper body out over the boots.

Basic swing turn   Once the basic idea of skidding the skis in a parallel swing has been grasped, then it is possible to use it as the latter half of a snowplough turn. By making turns starting with a narrow snowplough, and turning the inside leg and ski to match the outer steering ski when the skis are facing downhill, both legs flex and rotate to skid the skis back across the slope in a parallel swing. Now you can start your turns with a small angled-out snowplough. Then, when you are safely steering the outer ski, flex the legs and steer the rest of the turn with the skis parallel, using both edges to steer and brake. As you build up more confidence at making the basic plough-swing turns and allowing the skis to move faster, it will become possible to

develop a more sequential pattern to the movements you make when changing direction down a ski-run.

This is the stage in learning when the basic control skills should be done without thinking too much about them. You should have a good feeling for balance, and not make too many falls. You should also be able to move your weight over from ski to ski and apply steering pressure, as well as feel when the skis are edged or skidding.

Your skiing standard will now enable you to make descents down Blue-marked runs of moderate difficulty. These are served by automatic Poma Lifts that have a quicker take-off than practice lifts for elementary-standard skiers. Look at the signs and any directional lights that tell you how and when the lift operates, and be ready at the get-off point to move out of the way quickly! On the way down, look when overtaking other skiers, and give them a wide berth to avoid collisions.

Stem swings   The basic swing can be refined to moving only the upper ski out onto its inside edge as a small plough or stem. Practice is now the main concern to get an instinctive feeling for the skis and their control, so that all your turns finish with the skis skidding round the slope back into a traverse, as a parallel swing. The aim now is to steer more and more of the turn with the skis matched together, parallel.

The uphill stemming movement of the ski is made by a sliding step-out on to the inside edge – making the ski instantly ready to have the weight turning pressure shifted on to it, by stepping off the lower ski. The action becomes a linked sequence of movements: (1) step out, (2) step together, (3) flex down the legs and steer the skis into the new turn, bringing the skis into the parallel swing much earlier than in the basic plough swing.

The Italian Alberto Tomba makes a fast turn in the super giant slalom.

You may notice, as you travel up a lift and watch other skiers skimming down the runs alongside, that the better skiers use their ski poles when making turns. This is the stage in your skiing where the pole can be planted in the snow at the moment you make your turn.

In the stem swing the downhill hand reaches forward to plant the pole as support for stepping the lower ski in parallel, making a positive weight transfer to the new steering ski. It helps to flex the legs down as the pole is swung forward, so that the step off the lower ski is made by stretching the leg as the weight pressure is moved across.

Co-ordinating these movements to trigger off your turns now becomes the key to performing smooth-linked turns as you ski down. As you go, look for parts of the ski-run that enable you to link several turns together with a quickening tempo.

Basic parallel turning   A few years ago the ultimate goal was to become a proficient parallel skier, and it took many hours and ski holidays to get anywhere near a fluent standard. Now, with well-designed equipment and 'pisted' ski runs, it is much quicker for a learner skier to begin turning the skis in some form of basic parallel form.

This is now the objective for the student skier – to try and make all turns with the skis more or less parallel throughout the change of direction and linking one parallel swing into the next as a series of smooth rhythmic turns. However, it is necessary to understand that parallel turning has one essential difference to the type of turning technique learned so far. This centres on the change of the edges used for steering. When a turn is started by a plough or stem, the steering edge is changed one leg at a time as a stepping sliding action. In a parallel turn both edges are changed together, a simultaneous action of rotating the legs and changing the edges.

To help this simultaneous leg rotation and edge-change, weight is momentarily taken off the skis. Unweighting the skis is done by

The stem swing – stem the uphill ski to start turning then immediately close the inside ski into a parallel swing

flexing down the legs and then quickly extending up and forward over the balls of the feet. If you make this action with a sudden rise upward, the ski tails will lift off the snow. It is during this upward extension of the body that the legs and feet are rotated to turn the skis downhill.

You can settle down again after tilting the skis over onto their new edges and transferring turning pressure to the new steering outer ski. Use the pole to aid the unweighting and pivoting of the legs. Remember to bring the arm smoothly forward to plant the right pole to turn to the right, the left pole to turn left, always comfortably reaching to the downhill side as the legs make their first flex down ready to unweight the skis.

TECHNIQUE

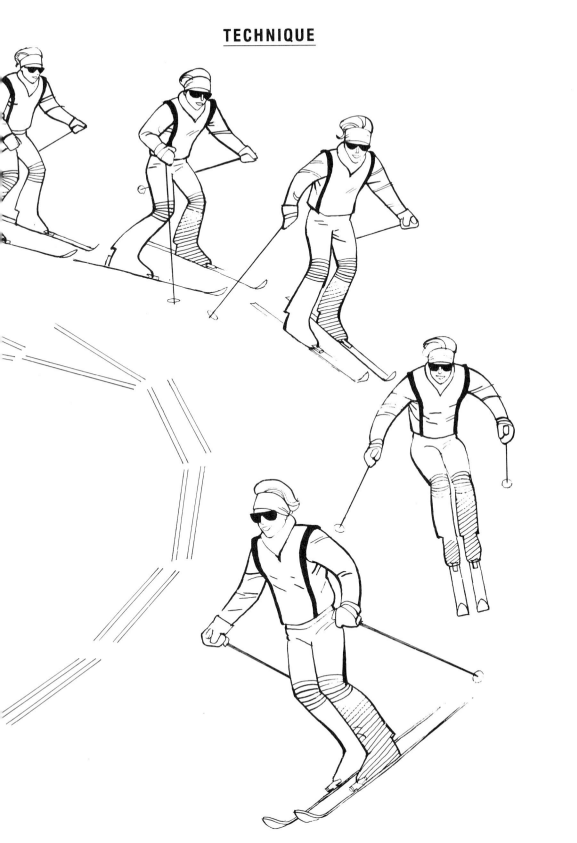

SKIING

Basic parallel turn, using
unweighting action to
turn both legs and skis

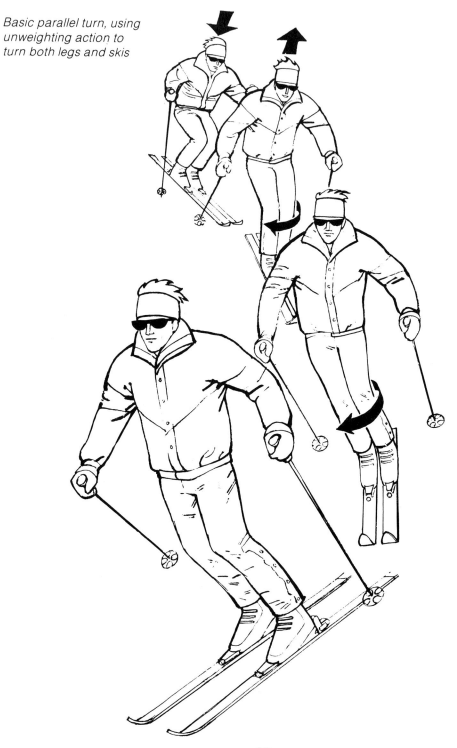

TECHNIQUE

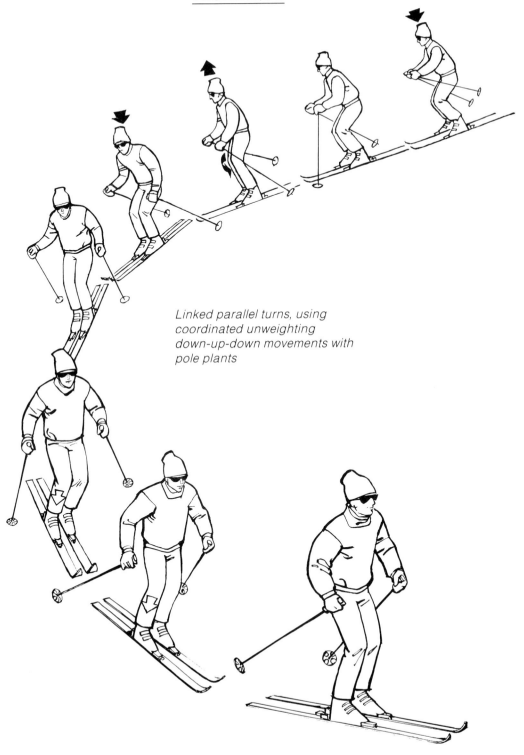

Linked parallel turns, using
coordinated unweighting
down-up-down movements with
pole plants

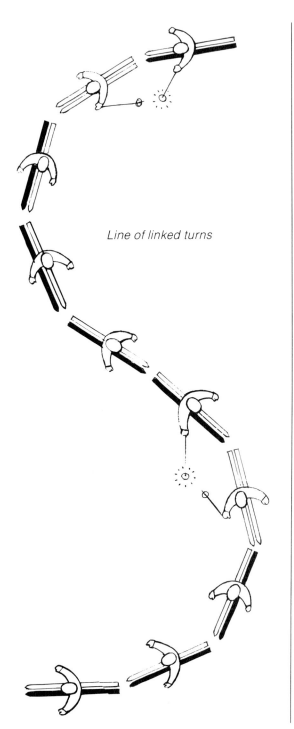

Line of linked turns

Co-ordination of the turning movements is important to make a smooth initiation of the skis into the parallel swing. From an open-stance 'ready position,' flex down with both legs, plant the pole, and extend up and unweight, rotate the legs, change the edges and weight the outer ski, settle down and steer the skis through the parallel swing.

Parallel skiing is all in the start of the turn when the skis are quickly changed over into a new swing direction. Being prepared in the 'ready stance' is crucial to getting all the leg action and pole plant correctly timed together. Get the feel of this action by traversing across a gentle slope, timing leg flex and pole plant to unweight the skis, without turning the legs. Co-ordination of these movements is the key to making parallel turns efficiently.

Once you have mastered the techniques to link turns together (either stemming one ski at a time or in basic parallels), then you have time to think of heightening your senses for everything involved in skiing.

Look for the best line or snow conditions, and for any ice or bumps that need avoiding. Listen for the sounds of skiing, the rush of air past you and the noise your skis make on the snow. Make yourself aware of the feeling for the skis and the snow, where you are pressing down on your feet, holding the pole snugly and the degree of pressure and edge-angle on the skis. These are just some of the many feelings that can add to your experience, bringing on an awareness that will improve your skiing.

Skiing is all about instinctive fluid movements; flexing and extending the legs to absorb the shocks of the terrain, and being ready to slow down, turn or change direction at any moment. This is the dynamic state of the skier in motion – correctly balanced, in control and using all the senses – not only skiing linked parallel turns smoothly, but also using other techniques as the situation arises.

SKI · SCHOOL

Ski schools have been a traditional part of skiing from the beginning of the sport as a holiday recreation. There are several advantages to joining a class, apart from the obvious fact that the instructor is trained to teach the fundamental skills of skiing progressively. There is the fun and enjoyment of being part of a group all in the same 'boat' trying hard to master the skis and meeting new people. Also, while it may seem tempting to learn from friends and other helpful 'expert' skiers, their advice may not necessarily be correct. Indeed it could well be out of date and lead you into all kinds of bad habits! "Watch me and try and do what I do" is not a recommended way to start you off. It is much better to start under the guidance of the ski school instructor who knows exactly how to look after the learner.

Ski schools are usually divided into six main class groups, from beginners through to the more expert top classes, with morning and afternoon sessions. Absolute beginners are advised to stay with each learning session, whereas someone who already has some skiing experience may take single class sessions leaving time to go and practise afterwards. All ski schools will arrange private tuition, which can be shared with a small group of the same standard.

The ski instructor's job is to explain and demonstrate clearly the movements of skiing, at the right speed. By breaking down the techniques into easily digested parts, the process of learning to control the skis becomes less complex as each new skill is introduced. The instructor also chooses the best snow slopes for the beginner to practise each stage, accurately guiding you through various exercises so you avoid picking up mistakes and begin to feel the skis correctly.

To get the best out of a ski class it is necessary to look and listen to the instructor carefully. Don't be distracted by the activity all round. In particular watch how the demonstration is made. Much of learning to ski comes from the visual image presented to you as the instructor shows you the movements, reinforced by any technical points that need explaining. Your practice then becomes a matter of 'copying' your instructor's movements and 'skiing shape.' Look at how others ski, and note the mistakes the other folk in the class make. Join in the laughs generated from everybody's efforts and struggles to remain in charge of the skis!

When the instructor is leading the group on a practice run, make sure that you get your turn immediately behind him or her for a clear view of where turns are made and a good image to copy of the instructor's movements. Being at the back of the line all the time puts you too far away to see exactly where the instructor is going, and the way in which the turning techniques are used.

Other disadvantages arise if the group is a large one. A lot of time can be spent waiting for stragglers or for your turn to perform a certain exercise – even more frustrating if the instructor has a limited command of English. Do try to get your share of the instructor's attention. If this doesn't seem to be happening, see the ski school chief and ask for a change of class.

A well-presented instructor who patiently leads you through the intricacies of learning to ski – making the lessons safe and enjoyable – is the highpoint of any beginner's skiing holiday. If this is not the case then you have reason to make representations to the tour operator or the ski school.

Artifical slopes Dry ski slopes have made learning to ski possible for many people, especially children, who would not have the opportunity to get onto real snow conditions. In addition, these slopes are extremely useful for good skiers to get fit and remain in practice with the latest techniques. In Great Britain there are slopes located close to all the large populated areas. They are open at various times through the day and evenings for sessions which are usually booked on an hourly basis.

Most slopes consist of a nylon-bristle matting served by some form of mechanical ski-tow system. The larger slopes have their own nursery areas to the side of the main slope. The material is not quite as slippery as snow but the techniques learned are exactly the same. Use your own boots if you have them, but use the slope's rental skis. Wear comfortable old clothing that can take the abrasions of falling on the matting, and have a pair of good-sized mitts to protect your thumbs and fingers.

Check with the slope operators for learning course sessions that may finally offer a holiday on snow either in Scotland or the Alps.

Ski Tows and Lifts

Apart from the obvious benefit of mechanical transportation uphill, using tows and lifts enables the skier to make several downhill runs in a relatively short time.

Being able to take several ski runs, without the effort of climbing back up, affords the kind of practice that is needed to consolidate and perfect the ski technique. However, as using lifts is all part of the process of learning to ski, there are certain guidelines you should be aware of.

Ski lifts basically come in two forms: those that you ride wearing your skis, like skiing uphill, and those that are used either sitting or standing, with skis taken off. The latter types of lift require no special instructions for

The baby tow

use, but riding lifts and tows with skis on needs care and attention.

Nursery training tows – these short simple tows serve the easy training areas on the nursery slopes. They can be just a rope to hold onto or grab handles or some form of "button" attached to the cable.

T-bar tows – serve longer runs and have retractable T-shaped bars fastened to the overhead cable. They are designed to carry two skiers up side by side.

Using the T-bar

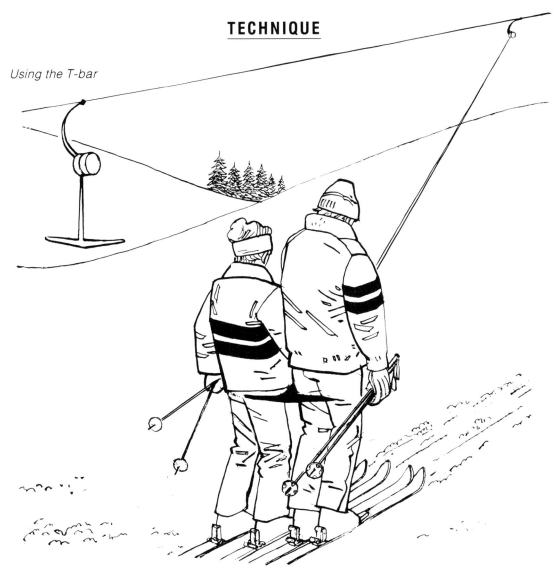

Using these lifts requires skiers to wait their turn and then carefully move into position. You should point the skis up the track and be ready to take hold of the bar and place it under the bottom, ready for the take-off pull. On a T-bar, try and choose a partner of roughly the same height so that the bar "sits" evenly between you. Hold the ski poles in your outside hand.

Poma lifts – have a single spring-loaded button pole attached to the cable which can be automatically dispensed to the skier at the starting off point. These tows have a design feature enabling them to go round corners, making siteing of the uphill track more flexible than the straight up T-bar track.

The Poma button is slipped between the legs, holding onto the bar ready for the pull uphill. On the ride uphill, all the skier has to do is steer the skis up the track. It is considered "bad form" to do slalom wiggle turns up the track, as this can unship the lift cable off the pulleys.

The getting-off point at the top will have

direction signs for the exit. Move quickly away once the bar has been let go, leaving the space clear for the next skiers.

Using chairlifts – follow a similar careful procedure at the get-on and off points. At the get-on point look back to see when the chair is arriving, reach out a hand to steady the chair as you sit down. Once underway, keep your ski tips clear of the snow and place the safety bar into position. The top will have an exit ramp to slide down, away from the chair, as soon as you stand up. Again, signs will indicate when you should be ready to get off.

Gondola lifts and cable cars – these are

aerial cableways that require no special instructions. The skis are taken off and you either sit down or stand up in the cabin for the journey to the top of the mountain.

Important note
When using all lifts and tows, read the instruction and direction signs before proceeding uphill, so that you understand exactly what to do and which runs the lift serves. In busy resorts, there are often two or more lifts run close together. One of these may go much higher on the mountains than you want. Check first which lift is the one you need.

The Poma lift

TECHNIQUE

The chairlift exit ramp

ON THE
PISTE

The Alpine snow-game of skiing, in its full sense, incorporates several factors that make it into the art of 'total skiing'. Ski technique is a necessary part of the sport, but it is only an introduction to the whole game. You must also develop an awareness of other external factors, such as weather and various hazards. Then use each run to the best advantage so that the skis and the mountain work for you to result in a total skiing experience.

The Craft of Total Skiing

Every ski-run has its own characteristics which are easily recognized. The slopes change their shape as the run follows the contours of the mountainside, over open ground, through wooded glades, by rocky outcrops and gullies, or simply down undulating alpine slopes. While most runs are 'pisted' down, the snow groomed and packed into a wide path by mechanical tracked vehicles nicknamed 'piste-bashers', there are points to look out for on the terrain which can be used to apply technique to your advantage, making skiing more pleasurable. On the other hand there are hazards which have to be recognized well before skiing on to them so that avoiding action can be taken.

Using the snow to your advantage means training your eye to look for the most obvious rounded humps which can be used

to turn your skis. Basic swings or parallel turns are made by steering the skis around the crest. The skis swing easily round the shape of the bump to change direction.

Look ahead to choose the best areas of snow on which to ski and particularly where to make your turns. Plant your pole on the rounded humps to trigger off a parallel swing around the slope. If the slope steepens off below the hump, allow the skis to skid in a broad swing to brake and control your speed. Sometimes the snow in the centre part of the run can become too hard-packed. However, down the sides loose snow may be lying to make steering easier and give a better feeling grip of your skis to link turns together. Scooped out gully-shaped sections provide fun skiing swooping up the sides. Take care if you have to overtake slower skiers.

When a piste run takes a bend look for smoother snow on the outside edge; faster skiers will cut the inside corner, creating deep grooves. Take a high track line around the outside. The long way round will keep you clear of the bumpy cut-off grooves on the inner side of the bend and the chance of loose snow is better toward the outer edge.

Long rounded ridges down the piste are also fun to ski down by linking turns along the crest, 'pivotting' the skis as they cross the crest just as when over a single hump.

Where the piste narrows to enter a bridge or a traversing ski road around the hillside,

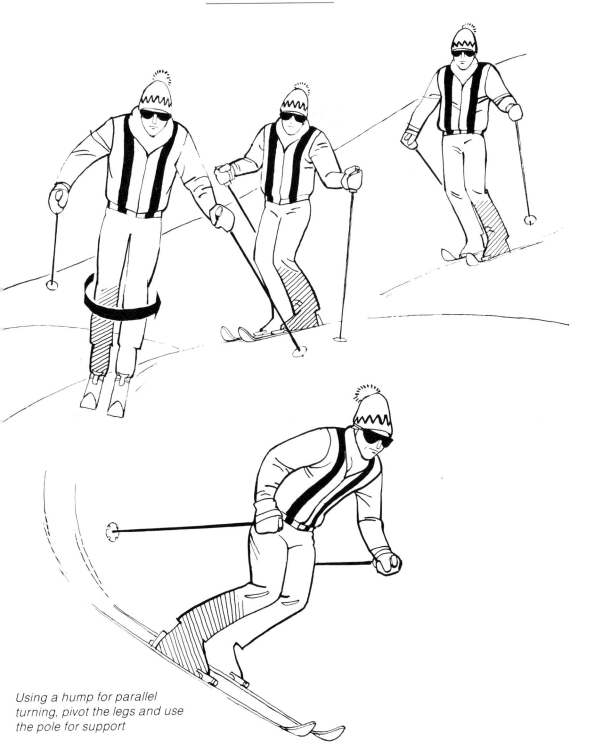

*Using a hump for parallel
turning, pivot the legs and use
the pole for support*

take a wide turn to ski onto the flat section from the side, not by a short cut into a sharp turn on the corner. This way you will control your speed, steering the skis directly into the opening and adjusting your balance to the sudden change from the slope to flat snow.

The hazards on the piste   Having given advice on the way to seek out the best parts of the piste, so that a route can be continually selected for the most enjoyable skiing, what about the hazards that need to be avoided? Snow conditions can vary and are not always 'user friendly.' Changes in the shape of the terrain create awkward pitches – weather conditions can have an overriding influence on visibility, governing skiing speed.

Difficult snow conditions   Probably the most unfriendly to skis and skiers is ice or polished hard snow. This usually shows up as dark patches and should be given a wide berth. If they cannot be avoided, try to relax and lower your centre of gravity by sinking down lower than the normal stance – use both skis to edge in a wide stance. Obviously to get the best grip, your ski edges should be sharp; dull edges or old skis that are losing their flex will not give the same control. Any movements you make to control the skis should be smooth and not sudden or hard. Tensing up results in the skis skidding off their edges, losing the positive angulated posture over the skis necessary to maintain the correct pressure down onto the skis. However, even on large areas of hard, icy-snow conditions, there are small areas where the surface has a roughened texture, giving a grip for turning.

Frozen ruts and hard lumpy crust   Any uneven surface has to be treated with care, as the skis are easily knocked off line and can be trapped in deep ruts. When there have been thaw conditions producing churned up snow, an overnight frost will produce a surface similar to a ploughed

field, unless it has been pisted down by the machines. Again, look for the smoothest patches on which to turn, stepping or hopping the skis quickly round to change from one traverse line to the next. Try to hold a flexible stance to absorb all the knocks and shocks as the skis ride over the lumpy surface.

Wet heavy snow   In the late season the gradual weathering of the snow produces the coarse granular 'spring snow' which gives some of the best skiing conditions. With strong sunlight, however, this can turn to deep mush as the day progresses, getting deeper and heavier in the afternoon as legs get tired. Making turns through this heavy snow requires the application of strong rotational pressure with both legs to prolong steering of the skis – almost like punching the tips through the deeper patches of mush with the knees. It requires a lot of energy to ski continuously through heavy snow, and care should be taken before your legs give out. Look to the sides of the piste where there may be more firm snow just under the surface, and where less skiing traffic will have churned up the snow.

Wind-blown drifted snow   Strong winds can blow masses of snow into sheltered areas, such as hollows and the lee-side slopes and ridges. The wind packs it into a dense, compact mass, easily recognized by the full flour-like surface texture. As the ski cuts into snow it breaks up in slabby chunks, and the skis will only go in a straight line, resisting your efforts to push them sideways. Turning in this type of dense snow is extremely difficult and should be treated with great caution. Step the skis out of the snow one at a time to slow down or change direction. This is the snow that produces slab avalanches if the slope is steep enough and the underlying layers are unstable.

New deep snow cover   Skiing through deep new powder snow is the dream of

A dramatic shot of the Norwegian skier Atle Skaardal in action.

many skiers, and although it is used extensively to advertise skiing in the glossy brochures, very few skiers ever get to ski in really deep powder. A moderate new snowfall of 6–8in (15–20cm) can be skied using normal techniques, once you have got accustomed to the extra resistance to the skis as they run inside the snow. Make all your turning movements with a little more exaggeration, waiting for the skis to start turning as they overcome the resistance of the snow.

Once the skis are turning, maintain the rotational pressure on the skis with the legs giving the skis time to steer through the snow. Any quick or jerky movements will affect the turning of the skis, causing one to dig deeper into the snow and do its own thing. Use a positive up-motion to unweight and start both skis into the turn.

The longer the snow lies and settles down, the more dense it becomes and turning the skis in the snow becomes more difficult. Care should be taken if you suddenly find that your skis are not reacting.

Variable snow cover   Where the snow is lying in a very thin cover, or has been worn down to the ground underneath, care should be taken to avoid hitting stones and rocks. In wooded glades, where snow conditions are variable and scraped thin, there may be tree roots on the surface that can be a hazard unless they have been planed down by the skiing traffic.

Rocks are bad news for ski soles, and should be avoided whenever possible. Step over or around them as soon as you spot them. Unfortunately, some rocks lie just under the surface, and when snow conditions are known to be of only a light cover, you should be doubly aware of the risk of catching your skis on a hidden rock. Be ready to step off the ski that is snagged. Deeper snow will always collect in hollows, so look for these spots if snow conditions are very marginal and you are searching for patches to ski down.

Difficult terrain   It is not always possible to find the particular line you would like. Inevitably as you progress to more difficult runs and ski trails there will be steeper pitches to negotiate on your way down. From above, steep slopes always look worse than they are. However, should you feel any anxiety at turning your skis down a steep pitch, slip across to lose height until you find a spot to turn.

Where there is a continuous steep line on a piste or trail, skiers control their speed by using their edges more, and making shorter turns. As a consequence of the repeated criss-crossing of turning on the same spots, the snow is gradually moulded into a pattern of grooves and bumps, called moguls.

Moguls   At first sight a mogul field of bumps looks very daunting, and if you ski on to them without care you will be bounced around and thrown off balance. Reading the best line to take through the bumps is the ultimate test of 'total skiing.' Look for the most rounded bumps that are well spaced apart. These are more than likely to be found down the edges of the mogul field. Moguls can be successfully negotiated by using the basic parallel turning technique utilizing bumps for the pivoting action when turning.

Ski steadily onto the crest of the bump and plant the pole for support as you swivel the skis around the crest. Timed correctly the skis will pivot easily as the centre of the skis under the boots is the only part in contact with the snow. Once the skis have turned, flex the legs to skid the skis down the outer slope of the bump, steering them toward the next crest.

In the hollows between the bumps, loose snow collects, making it possible to check your speed on these patches and give you time to choose the next mogul crest to pivot your skis around. The challenge of skiing down moguls is to continually look ahead to find the best line, keeping a positive attitude to controlled skiing over the humps and through the hollows.

Weather affecting visibility It is essential to see where you are going and if for any reason your vision is impaired, this will affect your ability to anticipate the terrain and snow conditions ahead. Overcast and misty weather produces flat light where all shadow disappears from the slope contours, making it difficult to see the humps and hollows. In complete white-out conditions the whole scene of snow and sky blends into one greyish mass, where even the downhill angle of the slope is extremely hard to register on your eye. If you are caught out in these poor light conditions, slow down your skiing speed accordingly so that you have time to feel for any changes in the shape of the slope. Wear goggles that will help to filter through the light and throw up any terrain features in relief, as well as trail markers that will save you from getting lost.

Skiing down wooded trails in brilliant sunlight, look out for the deep shadows cast across the run. Care should be taken as you ski into the shaded areas as it will be difficult to see uneven ground against the darkened surroundings, especially as the change on your sight may leave you with no time to adjust. In all situations of reduced visibility take up a more flexible stance over your skis, reduce speed and be ready to adapt your skiing as soon as you feel any changes in the terrain.

Have fun – but safely!

The total skier practises the skills and techniques learned for turning and controlling the skis by selecting the most friendly parts of the piste. Anticipate the terrain and the snow to give the most satisfying run down. At the same time develop a respect for the hazards to be avoided or treated with care, and always choose a sensible speed and skiing line which does not present you with unnecessary risks and difficulties.

Mogul absorbing technique

The total skier anticipates the terrain

Skiing with safety

Total skiing means that all skiers have to act responsibly and not recklessly bash down the piste, oblivious of other skiers and dangers. To help all skiers enjoy their sport in safety – using the pistes with regard to others, observing the natural hazards of the mountains in winter, and being aware of one's own limitations – a code of conduct has been drawn up.

The skiers' code of conduct

1. Consideration for others – you must ski in such a way that other skiers are not placed in danger.

2. Control of speed – a skier must ski in control always, adjusting their speed to be able to stop and avoid other skiers.

3. A slower skier has right of way – approaching another skier from behind, you must change your track to avoid endangering the slower skier.

4. Overtaking – overtake with a wide margin to avoid impeding the slower skier's

path (Note No. 3).

5. Stopping on the piste – a skier must avoid stopping, whenever possible, in the middle of a piste or narrow trail. Move to the side, as soon as possible, to ensure the safety and free passage of other skiers.

6. Walking or climbing up – when it is necessary to walk or climb near a piste, use only the side of the trail. Never walk or climb in the middle.

7. Joining a piste – the skier entering a main slope from an intersecting piste shall give way to skiers on the main slope.

8. Starting off – before starting off, or when crossing another track, look first to make sure the way is clear of other skiers.

9. All signs – observe and obey all piste signs placed to control downhill skiing and use of lifts. At all times co-operate with lift staff and Ski Patrol.

Personal check-list

● It is sensible to be physically fit before skiing. On the snow try to warm up before setting off. Wise skiers do a few stretching and limbering up exercises at the top of the lift before moving off downhill. This is very important if the weather is cold.

● Check that your equipment is correct and properly adjusted. Boots should fit correctly and skis/bindings should be in good order.

● Wear adequate clothing appropriate to the weather conditions and temperature at the top of the lift system.

● Check you have goggles or sunglasses, and use a recommended sun-cream and lipsalve for protection from sunburn in mountain-altitude conditions.

● It is not advisable to ski alone, better with companions or in ski school. Do not venture off the pisted tracks without an experienced guide, and always check that snow conditions are stable and not avalanche critical.

● Be aware of your own limitations. When cold or tired, stop for a while. Tired skiers and those who ski beyond their limits of ability are more prone to injury.

ON · THE · PISTE

International piste signs

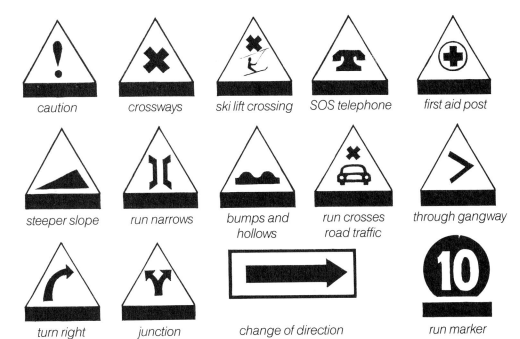

caution	crossways	ski lift crossing	SOS telephone	first aid post
steeper slope	run narrows	bumps and hollows	run crosses road traffic	through gangway
turn right	junction	change of direction		run marker

North American trail markings

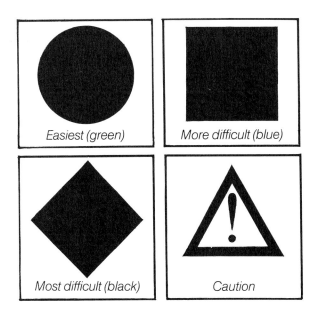

Easiest (green)	More difficult (blue)
Most difficult (black)	Caution

SKI CLINIC

Analyse the experts

Watch an expert ski down an undulating slope; it is a picture of effortless fluency. To achieve this proficiency the expert skier has had to learn by experience how to adapt ski technique to meet each new situation. Years of skiing practice will have helped develop a highly sensitive feeling for the skis, so the skier is always ready to make a change in direction according to the terrain, speed and snow conditions.

There are several points on which the average skier can learn to recognize where they are going wrong, work to eliminate errors and gradually acquire the graceful skill of the experts. Here are some movements to analyse for improved technique.

Parallel turning The expert is constantly adjusting the stance over the skis, in a **dynamically ready** position – flexed through all the joints, arms and poles held in balance, ready to change edges, steer, and allow the skis to ride smoothly over the snow. The minimum of effort is used to turn the skis. Unweighting action is barely noticeable because the expert uses the strong mechanical leverage of flexed legs to turn the skis. The upper body moves only enough to reinforce a weight pressure change and maintain the subtle shifts for balance control automatically.

Dynamic skiing

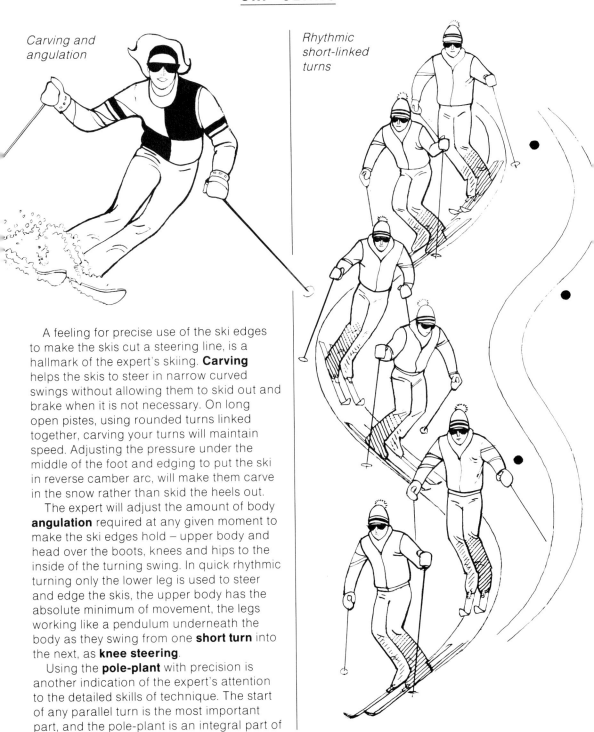

Carving and angulation

Rhythmic short-linked turns

A feeling for precise use of the ski edges to make the skis cut a steering line, is a hallmark of the expert's skiing. **Carving** helps the skis to steer in narrow curved swings without allowing them to skid out and brake when it is not necessary. On long open pistes, using rounded turns linked together, carving your turns will maintain speed. Adjusting the pressure under the middle of the foot and edging to put the ski in reverse camber arc, will make them carve in the snow rather than skid the heels out.

The expert will adjust the amount of body **angulation** required at any given moment to make the ski edges hold – upper body and head over the boots, knees and hips to the inside of the turning swing. In quick rhythmic turning only the lower leg is used to steer and edge the skis, the upper body has the absolute minimum of movement, the legs working like a pendulum underneath the body as they swing from one **short turn** into the next, as **knee steering**.

Using the **pole-plant** with precision is another indication of the expert's attention to the detailed skills of technique. The start of any parallel turn is the most important part, and the pole-plant is an integral part of

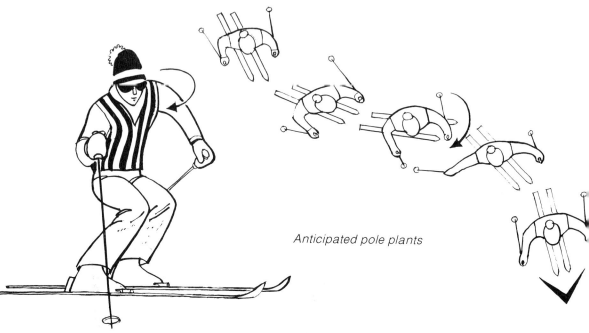

Anticipated pole plants

using the correct timing and co-ordination of the body's flexing movements. Correctly reaching forward to place the pole for support is the trigger into the parallel turn – pole planted close to the tip is for longer radius turns, gradually planting further back and away from the ski as the turns become shorter, and the terrain gets steeper. Placing the pole downhill from the body leads to an **anticipated** outward facing of the upper body. This pre-turning produces a twisting force through the legs when the edges are released – pivoting the skis while using the pole-plant for support.

Terrain skiing Using the terrain for turning is very much part of the way in which the expert adapts parallel techniques. **Absorbing** the humps and bumps by allowing the legs to fold up under the body as the skis cross over the crest, then stretching down as the skis slide into the hollows. Turning on the tops, as learned in basic parallel skiing, the expert has no need to unweight the skis, simply pivoting the skis round as the legs are compressed. **Mogul skiing** requires fitness and good reaction, but the same principle of absorbing the bumps is used, only the linking of turns becomes much more active and a quick eye

to read the skiing line – either through the hollows or over and around the bumps. The pole-plant is again important for support when turning the skis. Plant it near the crest so that as the boots come on to the top, the skier can then use it for stability while the legs are rotated and then extended down into the next hollow.

Looking at World Cup Racers on TV you will notice how they are continually stepping from one ski to the other – changing from one line to the other through the Control Gates. **Step turning** is not the sole preserve of the racing skier, it is used by the expert skier to make a positive change of steering ski edge. From the completion of one parallel swing, the uphill ski is stepped out to the side with the leg flexed, immediately followed by transferring steering pressure to this ski and planting of the pole on the downhill side.

The stepping sequence is completed by lifting in the lower ski as the parallel swing phase begins to steer the skis in the normal way. Quick changes of direction can be made using the step turn, even accelerating your speed by **skating** off the lower ski with a more energetic action. It is a good way of warming up on those first few turns in the morning.

Step turns

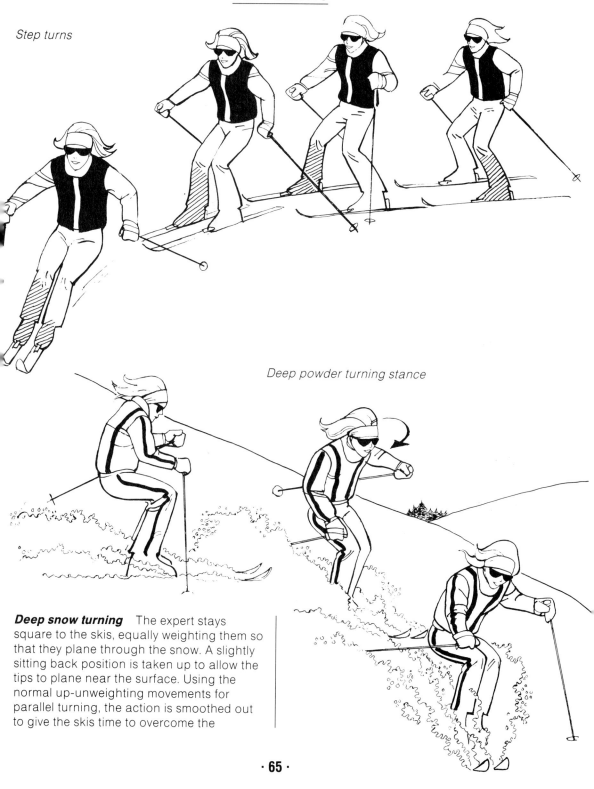

Deep powder turning stance

Deep snow turning The expert stays square to the skis, equally weighting them so that they plane through the snow. A slightly sitting back position is taken up to allow the tips to plane near the surface. Using the normal up-unweighting movements for parallel turning, the action is smoothed out to give the skis time to overcome the resistance of the snow as they turn. As the skis are steered downhill, both weighted, the skier banks to the inside of the turn to maintain equal turning pressure on both skis. It is a new feeling to acquire as there is no hard edging of the skis, and requires time to get accustomed to the 'floating' feeling of the skis.

Ski Clinic Fault Diagnosis

Skiing involves the learning of movements and changes of posture while in a sliding motion over the skis. Some of these movements are not instinctively natural and require instruction to acquire the correct feeling. Outlined here are some of the mistakes made when progressing through the fundamental stages of learning to ski.

General stance in motion   Too upright and stiff, no flexibility. Sitting back on heels, using the back of the boots for support.
Remedy Bring your arms and hands forward where you can see them out of the corner of your eyes. Feel your shin pressing on the front of the boot. Ski in rhythmic bounces to get flexibility.

Skidding in the traverse   Leaning in to the slope, stiff lower leg and ski not holding a tracking line.
Remedy Advance the uphill ski at least half a boot length. Reach out downhill with the outside arm, knees in to the slope for edge grip. Check that your head is immediately over the lower boot.

Snowplough overturning   Stiff outer steering leg, rotating inwards with the shoulders, plough angle too wide with tips too far apart.
Remedy Check the plough angle, tips together. Flex the turning ski leg, knee toward the ski tip. Reach out to the side with your arm, or bring the inside hand across the body to touch the outside steering leg knee.

Unable to make a basic swing   Reluctance to steer both skis parallel, holding onto both inside edges for stability. Rotating upper body to the inside of the swing, stiff outer leg.
Remedy Flexing down movement of both legs, sliding the inside ski forward to change the edge, feel for a positive weight change to the outer ski.

Stem parallel turn   Stemming habit at the start of the turn, shuffling across from one ski to the other; insufficient flex down and up extension movements to unweight both skis; poor use of the pole-plant.
Remedy Make an emphasized downflex to edge both skis before the turn start. Plant the pole on the downhill side at the same time. Push off with both legs to flatten and turn the skis while they are temporarily unweighted. Transfer the weight to the uphill ski as early as possible, always followed by a smooth downflex to steer the skis into the swing. Use exercise hops side to side to feel both skis moving as one unit.

Poor pole-plant   Over-reaching and swinging of the pole too far forward. Too late with the pole, after the skis have turned.
Remedy Swing the pole forward by wrist action to plant just back from the ski tip. The pole hits the snow before the skis are turned, as the legs make the preparatory sinkdown. Practise the movements in the traverse to get the timing right.

Linked turning – poor rhythm   Splitting of the skis, heels skidding out, over-rotating of the upper body. Poor timing of the pole-plant.
Remedy Stabilize the upper body, face down the slope all the while. Keep both hands in sight reaching downhill, push off outer ski to turn both legs under the body in rhythmic timing with the pole plant.

Ingemar Stenmark – the most successful slalom ski racer of all time

Do I need to wax my ski soles?

The Polyurethane low friction base will have the sliding quality improved by waxing – melt on and scrape down smooth. The block waxes are colour coded – Red for wet snow, Blue for below freezing and Neutral for general snow conditions.

Is a special skiing holiday insurance necessary?

It is important to be covered for accident, rescue facility costs and any hospitalization, as well as any accident involving a third party. Comprehensive insurance is available which covers other extras such as travel and ski equipment.

I am prone to cold hands and feet, what is the answer?

Use mitts rather than gloves and piled knit ski socks.

What is the correct feeling of fitting, when wearing boots?

With all the clips closed, there should be some flex of the leg above the ankle, but the heel should be held down snugly with the toes free to move.

If I can't understand what my instructor is saying, what should I do?

Look very carefully at the demonstration of the exercises or turns that the instructor makes, do not be distracted – try and get an image imprinted in your mind, of the technique required, and then try to copy the same movement.

Is there any age limit for learning to ski?

So long as you are generally physically sound, you can take up skiing at any age. With shorter skis and correct instruction to take the "mature citizen" into account, there is no reason why you cannot enjoy skiing just as much as a teenager.

As a beginner into skiing, how long will it take to become a proficient parallel skier?

Much depends on your fitness and feeling for balance. On average it takes three or more ski holidays to get into parallel turning. On the other hand, there are some skiers who can make basic parallels after only one week of tuition.

What are the benefits of joining a ski club?

Apart from the social aspects of a club's meeting programme, there are benefits from discount holidays, equipment, group training sessions and club racing.

What makes Nordic Skiing so popular?

It is particularly interesting to people who already enjoy walking and mountaineering, or who are keen runners, orienteerers or cyclists. However, the sport is cheaper all-round, and because of the lighter equipment, simpler bindings and slower speed, it is very safe and gives all-round exercise.

At what age are children ready to go into ski school?

Unless the ski school has a kindergarten area for small children, most ski schools prefer children to be from 6–7 years old before learning.

How can a keen junior skier begin ski racing?

Joining a ski club will enable the aspirant racer to have the chance to take part in organized training and coaching, giving encouragement and guidance into the racing programme.

Is it possible for the average D.I.Y. enthusiast to repair and service their own skis?

Yes, refer to the various articles in current ski magazines on maintenance advice. Ski shops stock repair kits and edge-sharpening files.

Is it wise to use a ski-locking device when parking my skies at lunchtime?

Unfortunately, stealing skis from outside cafes and even hotel lockers is a social disease that is prevalent in some ski resorts. A lightweight lock and cable will deter ski thieves, especially if two or three pairs are locked together.

When skiing down the trail or ski-piste, who has the right of way?

The faster skier must give way to the slower skier – overtaking with as wide a margin as possible.

As a learner skier on holiday with friends, do I have to take a whole day's instruction?

Once you have the basic skills of technique, then you can take lessons in the morning sessions and ski with friends after lunch.

How should I store my ski equipment, once the winter is over?

Unlike the old days when skis had to be clamped up to keep their shape, modern skis just need to have a protective waxing on the soles and edges and be clipped together. Check poles for any repair. Dry out boots thoroughly and store in a dry loft or locker.

Is it worth buying special clothes for my first skiing holiday?

Yes – trousers, jacket, thermal underwear, socks and hat. No – boots.

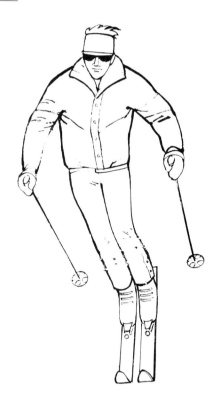

Is it a good idea to try skiing on a dry slope before booking my skiing holiday?

Yes. This can help you to get the feeling of wearing skis and understanding basic techniques. However, it is a much slower surface and is harder to fall on than real snow.

What sort of resort is best for beginners?

Check with your travel agent about which resorts offer good tuition and have shorter, easier runs that are suitable for beginners.

What happens if there is no snow in our resort?

If you are on a package holiday, you should be taken to somewhere else suitable in the area.

SKIING

What can I do to minimize the aches and pains after my first day?

Try to avoid this happening by doing pre-ski exercises before you go. If you do get aches and pains, take a hot bath after skiing to relax those tensed-up muscles.

Pre-Ski Exercises

Before going on a ski holiday it is wise to be as fit as possible. You need to be prepared for physical activity which may involve muscles and joints in positions that you do not normally use. For the beginner the first time on snow will mean falling down and getting up again, which can be demanding on muscles that are unused. Without some exercise preparation beforehand, it is possible to become stiff and ache all over after only a couple of days into a holiday. While it is not necessary to train as if going

in for a marathon, making the effort to get into some reasonable physical shape reduces the risk of strains and becoming over-tired.

The exercise programme suggested here is designed to cover both a general body tone-up and simulated exercises of the common movements made in skiing. Supplemented by the awareness of a healthy diet, a simple exercise programme (including regular cycling, walking, jogging or swimming) will benefit everyone and make your ski holiday more enjoyable.

● **Arm stretch** – stand upright with knees and feet together. With palms facing up, stretch arms sideways. Swing arms back and hold. Relax and repeat several times.

● **Knees bend** – in the same position as arm stretch, and keeping feet on floor, bend and rise gently several times. Try to bend lower each time, keeping back straight.

Arm stretch

Knees bend

● **Thighs alive** – sit with back flat against a wall, knees bent at right angles. Hold position for 30 seconds. Increase time as your strength builds.

● **Leg raising** – sit in a chair and hold the underside of it firmly with both hands. Raise your legs until horizontal and hold. Lower them gently.

● **Squat jumps** – in the half squat position, jump forward, back and then to either side.

● **Arm and body circles** – with the feet apart, circle arms slowly forward from shoulder, then repeat with arms going backwards. With hands at side revolve upper body, followed by hip circles, as with hoop.

● **Back exercise** – lie face down on the floor with arms clasped behind you. Pull your upper body into an arched position and hold for a few seconds. Relax and repeat three times.

Thighs alive

Back exercise

Leg raising

SKIING

● **Deep knee side press** – alternate side to side, press both knees right and left rolling over on the soles of the feet.

● **Snowplough knee press** – feet apart, toes in, press down on alternate legs, stretching up to change over. Hands on hips.

Stretching exercises on the snow:
● **Trunk twist to right and left** – hold poles together behind shoulders, twist to face the side steadily.

● **Alternate leg slide and stretch** – push alternate knee forward as a stretching slide, reach forward and back with opposite arm action.

● **Turn and reach down** – Skis well apart, arms out to the side, twist and reach down, right hand to touch left boot, left hand to right boot.

● **Side-step up a few metres,** then begin your skiing by vigorously bouncing in the turns, or using a quick stepping movement from ski to ski.

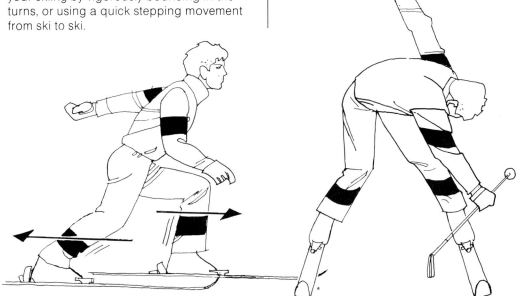

Trunk twist

Alternate leg slide and stretch

Turn and reach down

RESORT ROUND-UP

Skiing has spread throughout the world — anywhere there is snow, a hillside and people who want to ski, lifts are built and a ski area developed. From the mini ski areas on the eastern side of North America to the high Himalayas, there are lift-served ski slopes. Instructors from the northern winters travel south to the mountains of Australia, New Zealand and South America in the summer months to work in ski schools in the developing resorts of the southern hemisphere.

The European Alps, however, are still the most popular winter playground for the holiday skier, with the mountain regions of North America also offering extensive skiing facilities.

Most resorts have development programmes for improving the service provided for skiers. Lift systems are continually being modernised, replaced or added to for the increasing number of skiers, in order to reduce waiting time and open up new slopes. Pistes and ski trails receive attention in the closed season, widening and smoothing out the ground to make skiing safer. Hotels have updated their facilities, and there are additional services and recreation activities on offer. The latest alternative snow sports of snowboarding and monoskiing are an example of the growth trend to try alternative sport.

The growing popularity of **Nordic Skiing** has made many resorts add cross-country trails and tracks as part of their skiing facilities. Cross-country skiing offers an inexpensive healthy activity for those who want to leisurely wander through pleasant undulating snowy terrain, or for anyone of any age who wants to test their competitive ability in Citizens Races. Summer skiing on glacier facilities is being extended in the higher Alpine areas, so that several ski resorts can now offer year-round skiing.

Austria – has the special welcoming charm of its Alpine Villages and the friendliness of mountain people. While the Eastern Alps are not as big as their neighbours, they offer much variety of skiing. The tradition of efficient ski schools and great après-ski are plus points to consider if Austria is your choice.

France – there have been many new ski resorts developed over the past few years through the French Alps and the Pyrenees mountains. They are specifically designed to cater for the mass of skiers, with efficient lift systems and wide pistes. Purpose-built modern resorts cannot have the charm of traditional Alpine villages, but do cater for the demands of the growth in skiing, particularly with linked resort lift systems.

Italy – the main resorts are concentrated along the Alpine borders in the north of the country. Most of these are old-estabished town resorts, but there are newly developed areas. The largest linked ski-lift circuit in the world is claimed for the connected resorts around the Dolomite Mountains. Costs in Italy are reasonable and the reliable weather in the southern Alps adds to its appeal.

North America – the Canadian and U.S. Rockies and Sierra Nevada mountain ranges have developed ski resorts, with the Rockies having some excellent powder snow conditions. Of particular interest is the growth in Heli-skiing – using helicopters to fly into inaccessible snow bowls. Friendliness and efficient chairlift service is the norm at all American resorts, with extra special care given to grooming the trails.

Scotland – development of ski facilities in the Scottish Highlands has lagged behind the growth in the number of skiers. However, when weather conditions are not extreme, the skiing is enjoyable in the 'corries' and deep gullies, with more holiday accommodation being made available in the valleys. The established resort of Aviemore remains the most popular area, with Glenshee and the new development of Aonach Mor, Fort William, offering equally good ski sport. Spring snow skiing in Scotland has much to recommend for late season sport.

Switzerland – the highest mountain areas of the Alps are reflected in any typical Swiss resort – solid, somewhat staid, but reassuringly efficiently organized. Switzerland offers the best and most challenging of skiing, but can be generally expensive. Endeavour to keep costs down by going where tour operators have established packaged holidays. Summer skiing on glaciers is available in many areas.

Franz Klammer shows the rugged style of a legendary downhill Olympic gold medal winner

USEFUL ADDRESSES

Europe:

British Ski Federation
258 Main Street
East Calder
West Lothian
EH53 0EE

Scottish National Ski Council
Caledonian House
South Gyle
Edinburgh EH12 9DQ

English Ski Council
6th Floor
Area Library Building
The Precinct
Halesowen
West Midlands B63 4AJ

Ski Council of Wales
240 Whitechurch Road
Cathays
Cardiff CF4 3HD

Northern Ireland Ski Council
House of Sport
Upper Malane Road
Belfast

British Association of Ski Instructors
Grampian Road
Aviemore
Inverness-shire PH22 1RL

Association of Ski Schools in Gt Britain
Abernethy Outdoor Centre
Nethybridge
Inverness-shire
PH25 3ED

Ski Club of Great Britain
118 Eaton Square
London SW1W 9AF

Scottish Ski Club
Mayview
Ardargie
Nr Forgandenny
Perthshire

North America:

Professional Ski Instructors of America
133 South Van Gordon
Suite 240
Lakewood
Colorado 80228 USA

Canadian Ski Instructors Allianc
3300 Cavendish Blvd.
Suite 350
Montreal
Quebec HB4 2M8 Canada

Details of ski schools, artificial slopes and special ski courses can be obtained from these addresses. Travel agencies will have information on packaged ski holidays.

CLINIC

INDEX

Figures in *italics* indicate illustrations

Michela Figini uses her elegant style to win World Cup races

INDEX

Figures in *italics* indicate illustrations